FLY LIKE AN EAGLE

Real Life Stories of Hope and Inspiration

Compiled by Gary Doi

Fly Like an Eagle is an anthology of real life stories of hope and inspiration by twenty-six VIPs (Very Interesting People). The writers are everyday men and women from different parts of the world. They come from all walks of life. For example, a sixty year old grandmother who struggles with weight issues describes her first-time experience competing in a grueling athletic competition, the triathlon. A young teacher in Muscat, Oman who underwent successful surgery to remove a mass on the brain reflects on how that changed her perspective on life. A high tech manager in San Francisco asks and answers the question: What makes this city so great? A retired country doctor shares a remarkable story of how, as a fourteen year old, he underwent a blood transfusion to save his mother's life. A librarian on a service trip to Central America describes how greater access to books is helping vulnerable children in Guatemala. And, a mother writes a "Dear Jon" letter—a heartbreaking tribute to her son who died while on tour of duty in Afghanistan.

All of these short stories and more are true. They are deeply personal. They spawn moments of self-reflection. They probe the eternal question: What gives you hope?

Hope is the belief and aspiration to be better. Hope keeps us moving forward when dealing with life challenges that come our way. Hope gives us a sense of accomplishment and purpose.

Hence, the title *Fly Like an Eagle*. An eagle can reach great heights by soaring on thermals and then gliding long distances using the smallest amount of energy. To rise above circumstances. To soar.

Fly Like an Eagle follows on the heels of our first book, *Inspiring Hope: One Story at a Time*, published in 2013. Net proceeds from that book were used to hire a part-time librarian for Miguel Asturias Academy, a private, non-profit, Pre K-12 school serving vulnerable students in Xela, Guatemala.

Profits from *Fly Like an Eagle* will be donated to SORCO, a rescue, rehab and release facility (in the Okanagan region of BC) for raptors such as eagles, hawks and owls. Each year, this non-profit organization helps dozens of sick and injured raptors that were hit by vehicles, poisoned or found starving.

The artwork for the book cover and section dividers are courtesy of celebrated Canadian artist Roy Henry Vickers. Roy's graphic style painting combines dramatic aboriginal imagery with his passion and respect for the natural world. Thank you, Roy, for your generosity and friendship over the years.

Zee Gorman (from California) managed the online publishing process and I am immensely grateful for her leadership and assistance. She was a tremendous resource who provided a wealth of creative design ideas to the book.

I am also indebted to Kelowna writer Cathryn Wellner for editing several of the stories. She was always there to lend a helping hand.

Finally, a big thank you to all of the writers who so freely contributed their time, talent and personal stories. It is what makes this anthology so special. That like-minded people from different parts of the world can collaborate—in content, design and spirit—and produce something of interest to so many others.

Now that's hopeful and inspiring.

Gary Doi, October 2014

Echachis, Roy Henry Vickers

PREAMBLE

Kindness, beauty, quiet smiles, hardship, remembrances . . .
They are the kind of stories that lift your spirits and brighten a cloudy day.

Inspiring Hope: One Story at a Time

Published in 2013. Net proceeds were used to hire a part-time librarian for Miguel Asturias Academy, a private, non-profit, Pre K-12 school serving vulnerable students in Xela, Guatemala. Available for sale online at amazon.com, amazon.co.uk, and amazon.ca.

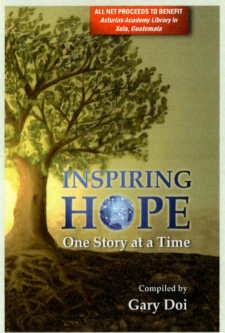

Fly Like an Eagle

Copyright © 2014 Gary Doi and authors listed on the CONTENTS page.

All rights reserved. No images, photos, graphics, texts or other materials in this book can be reprinted, reused, or reproduced without the permission of the authors. Opinions expressed by one author do not necessarily reflect the perspectives of the other authors.

Printed in U.S.A. in 2014.

This book can be purchased at www.amazon.com, www.amazon.co.uk, and www.amazon.ca

For inquiries contact garydoi@telus.net.

ISBN-13: 978-1502320148
ISBN-10: 1502320142

TO ALL THOSE WHO INSPIRE HOPE

CONTENTS

Fly Like an Eagle—GARY DOI	02

Dreams & Memories
Waiting for Diefenbaker—DARLENE FOSTER	06
The First Snow Fall—NINA MUNTEANU	09
Mother's Rebirth—STERLING HAYNES	12
The Washing and the Winnowing—DEBRA EVE	15
The Best Wedding Ever—CATHRYN WELLNER	18
Why San Francisco Stole My Heart—ZEE GORMAN	21
The Being There—JOHN MCLAUGHLIN	25
Memory and Mystery, Meaning and Magic—IAN LAWTON	28
Holiday Musings—ZEE GORMAN	32

Greater Good
Bringing It Home—SARAH DAHLEN	36
Rescuing a Red-tailed Hawk—DAVE WHITTON	39
The Kindness of Strangers—NANCY SATHRE-VOGEL	42
An Imperfectly Perfect Life Lesson—TARA RUMMELL BERSON	45
Be Great!—JENNIFER CACACI	48
Conducting Greatness—SHARON REED	51

New Heights
Stairway to Heaven—BRUCE MASTERMAN	56
Trust the Process—FRANCISCO LITTLE	59
Conquering Fears, Conquering Canyons—LEIGH MCADAM	63
I'm a Loser and I Love It—ARLA MONTEITH	66
Hear No Evil—GUY TAL	69
A Lifetime of Memories—LARRY OSACHOFF	72

Turbulence
The Sweet Scent of Home—GARY DOI	76
Patience…—AIMEE LEDEWITZ WEINSTEIN	80
When Tragedy Strikes—LAURA BEST	84
Self Portrait—CARRIE ELLEN BRUMMER	86
Dear Jon—ANNE SNYDER	89
Hope—SHARON REED	92
Laughter and Letting Go—CAROLYN SOLARES	93

The South Okanagan Rehabilitation Centre for Owls

Great Horned Owl chicks

Snowy Owl

Bald Eagle

ALL NET PROCEEDS FROM BOOK SALES will be donated to the South Okanagan Rehabilitation Centre for Owls (SORCO). Its mission is to rehabilitate injured and orphaned birds of prey (also known as raptors) and release them back into the wild. For more information, check out the website (www.sorco.org).

Fly Like an Eagle

By Gary Doi (Penticton, British Columbia)

Roy Henry Vickers

> **Rise above your circumstance. Soar. Reach new heights. Fly like an eagle.**

They are wonderful aspirations for life and living. They speak to a universal spirit of strength, truth and beauty. They challenge and inspire us to become better people.

Welcome to the world of Roy Henry Vickers, a Canadian artist of such prominence that his paintings and prints have been presented as official gifts from the Province of British Columbia to Queen Elizabeth II, Soviet leader Boris Yeltsin and U.S. president Bill Clinton. His work can be found in private and public collections and galleries around the world. He is also an accomplished carver, design advisor of public spaces, a sought-after keynote speaker, author of several popular books, a recognized leader among First Nations communities and a recipient of numerous awards including the Order of B.C. and the Order of Canada.

Roy was born into the Eagle clan. His father was a fisherman with the blood of Tsimshian, Haida and Heiltsuk First Nations flowing in his veins. His mother was of British descent and a schoolteacher in the native village of Kitkatla.

"Before my mother married my father," explained Roy, "the Kitkatla chief adopted her as his daughter, and she acquired the Eagle crest. This is an old Indian custom which gave my mother rank and status in the community. In the 1940s, a well-educated white woman marrying an Indian man had not been done."

Roy proudly carries his childhood with him. He has wonderful memories of growing up in northern BC, the home of his First Nations ancestry and heritage and the inspiration for his abiding passion for the beauty of the natural world. It is evident in who he is and what he does.

From an early age, Roy loved to draw. Any place and any time.

"I remember my teacher caught me drawing in her English class and, after school, I had to write lines on the blackboard," said Roy, smiling broadly. "With chalk in hand I had to write 100 times—I will not draw in English class. And then I'd have to rub it all off and clean the blackboard."

Roy moved to Victoria, BC to complete his high school education and after graduating took a job with the Saanich fire department while still pursuing his interest in art. In 1972, with the encouragement of friends, family and coworkers, he enrolled in a two-year First Nations art and design program at the Gitanmaax School of Northwest Coast Indian Art in Hazelton.

"It was love at first lesson," said Roy. "I immersed myself in the program and worked six days a week, 10-12 hours a day. My whole attitude toward my creativity changed. I knew it would be my profession and way of life."

In a relatively short period of time, Roy became one of the most prolific and popular artists in British Columbia. In 1986 he built (with the help of his family and legendary carver Henry Nolla) the Roy Henry Vickers' Eagle Aerie gallery located in Tofino, BC (www.royhenryvickers.com). It is a stunning, traditional Northwest Coast longhouse with a carved and painted cedar plank exterior and hand adzed interior walls along with four house posts, two Eagle and two Raven.

1992 was one of his most successful years as an artist. Gallery sales of paintings and prints easily reached over a million dollars that year. His list of supporters, customers and future projects was long and impressive. He had the King Midas touch.

However, unbeknownst to the public, Roy's personal life was in shambles. He was deeply troubled.

"My life was not a work of art," said Roy of that time period. "My life was hell. Unbearable. I had gone through two marriages and divorces. On Valentine's Day that year, I decided to end it all and sat alone in my house with the knowledge that I was no example for others to follow. The only thing that stopped me was my belief in God. He gave us life and we do not have the right to end it. I swore at God that if I knew of a way out of this, I would take it."

It was at that low point in his life when Roy's sister intervened. She talked with him about the harsh realities of addiction and suggested a way out. She recommended he call a recovery center in Arizona called "The Meadows".

Nine days later, Roy enrolled in the program.

"That was twenty-two years ago," said Roy. "Since that time, I have been working at recovery and discovering the strength, the truth and the beauty of who I am. It took me a long time to look in the mirror and say to that man—I love you."

Roy described how the recovery centre empowered him with some key lessons— the most important being that we have seven emotions.

"If we learn to process those emotions then there is no place for addiction," said Roy. "Alcohol, cigarettes and morphine are not addictive. The human mind is addictive. If we do not learn to process our emotions then we will suffer whatever will take us out of our emotions."

It was Roy's promise to himself as an artist—to always work from inspiration— which kept him alive.

"It was my life ring," said Roy. "Every time it felt like my world was crashing I would go to my artwork and come to this place of centeredness. I would create a beautiful image which came from somewhere inside me."

1992 may seem like a long time ago but not for Roy. It was the fundamental turning point in his life.

"You are what you think," explained Roy. "You live from your words as you act from those thoughts. So, how you think is your belief about the world and yourself. Now, I find the harder you work at being a good person, the more peace and happiness you have."

Those who are familiar with Roy's artwork will recognize his signature image, the stylized eagle.

"The eagle represents vision and freedom," said Roy. "It reminds humanity that the sky is the limit. It reminds us that with good vision and help from the Creator of all, we can soar with eagles. It reminds us that we can be free to explore high and far and to navigate the turbulence that life often brings."

Without a doubt, Roy is a changed man, someone who is comfortable within himself and free from addiction. In 2001 he married his best friend Andrea and purchased a house on eighty-seven acres in the Skeena River Valley, close to the town of Hazelton. Together, they share a wonderful, loving relationship with their two children.

Compiled by Gary Doi

As one of Canada's premier artists, Roy continues to create stunning graphic-style paintings and prints that combine aboriginal imagery with his passion and respect for nature. At age 68, Roy strives to improve each and every day. He is a consummate learner. Humble. Grateful. Giving. Open-minded. Caring. Motivated.

He truly knows what it means to rise above your circumstance.

To soar.

To reach new heights.

To fly like an eagle.

Story-telling with Roy Henry Vickers (Eagle Aerie Gallery, Tofino, BC)

Gary Doi served as Superintendent of Schools for eighteen years in three school districts in British Columbia. Previous to that, he was a teacher, consultant, school administrator and university lecturer. He created the magazine blog, "A Hopeful Sign" as he believes there is no greater force for creating change than hope. In 2013, he published the anthology "Inspiring Hope: One Story at a Time" to benefit a school library in Guatemala. "Fly Like an Eagle" is his second book dedicated to inspiring hope. Since retiring, Gary continues to pursue his interests in writing, golf, mountain biking, photography, travel, and volunteer work.

AUTHOR (ON THE RIGHT) WITH HER PRAIRIE FAMILY, 1959

WAITING FOR DIEFENBAKER

By Darlene Foster (Delta, British Columbia)

Back on the farm we learned a lot about hope. Dad hoped it would rain, that it wouldn't hail and destroy the crops, and for a good price when he sold his cattle. Mom hoped her garden would grow, the chickens would lay eggs, and we would keep the house clean after she slaved over it, just for once. As for me, I hoped for excitement and the opportunity to meet interesting and famous people. I wished for a brush with greatness.

Growing up on a prairie farm, I felt the world pass me by. Nothing exciting ever happened to me. Idle hours were spent daydreaming about visiting exotic places such as Paris, London, Rome or Regina. I longed to meet people in the news; interesting folks like Bobby Darrin, Debbie Reynolds, Gordie Howe or Prince Charles. I hoped in vain, since no one of consequence knew that the small town—or rather hamlet—near our farm, existed.

Things were about to change when I heard that John Diefenbaker, the Prime Minister of Canada, planned a visit to our placid little corner of the province. Mr. Diefenbaker, or Dief as he was fondly called, was a prairie boy and popular in these parts. It was an election year, and Dief sought another term in office. As was the custom at the time, he traveled across Canada by train, making whistle stops along the way. He intended to stop at all the major cities as part of his campaign.

The school buzzed with the news that Mr. Diefenbaker would stop for a short visit on his way through the following day. No one questioned why he would stop at our town, population of around 500, not counting gophers and coyotes.

My dream of meeting someone important was about to come true! I invited my girlfriend, Sharlene, to stay overnight so we could ride the bus in to school together the next morning. We got up early that memorable day, took the sponge rollers out of our hair, fixed our faces and put on our newest poodle skirts. The excitement in the school caused so much distraction that the teachers gave up trying to teach us anything. Truth be told, they were excited, too. The school closed at lunch and we all walked down to the train station in plenty of time to meet our special visitor.

Word spread. It looked as if everyone within a forty-mile radius showed up for this historic event. Cheerleaders in the school colours of white, black and gold shook their pompoms while they practiced a cheer for the P.M. School band members tuned their instruments. Farmers parked their trucks and tractors by the side of the road, wiped their faces with polka dot hankies, hitched up their dungarees and greeted neighbours. Young mothers, pleased to have a reason to escape the daily routine, pushed babies in buggies while toddlers trailed behind. Old folks located good viewing spots, unfolded their woven lawn chairs and relaxed as they waited. The Mayor, a kindly old man, went over his welcome speech with the School Principal, who took his wire-rimmed glasses on and off to get a better look at the handwriting. Sharlene and I made sure we were at the front of the railway platform, exactly where we thought our special guest would disembark. We planned to be the first to shake his famous hand.

According to our information, Mr. Diefenbaker was due to arrive at 1:00 p.m. A grade 10 student everyone called the Stick, kept track by ham radio.

"He's running ten minutes late. He should be here by 1:10," the Stick reported with a whiny voice.

At 1:05 my heart did flip-flops. I turned to Sharlene.

"Do I still have lipstick on? Is my hair in place?"

"You look great." She gave my hand a squeeze.

"Here it comes!" shouted the Stick.

In the distance, a speck of moving steel with a mane of black smoke was bringing our hero, the prime minister of the country, to our very doorstep. The iron horse grew larger and larger.

The cheerleaders stood in position, the bandleader lifted his baton, the mayor shuffled his notes, the principal put his glasses on, and Sharlene and I smiled our very best Doris Day smiles. We stepped closer to the tracks.

"He's not slowing down!" shouted the Stick.

The train whistle blew as the huge hunk of metal roared through the town. The noise deafened us. The platform vibrated under our feet and hot dust flew through the air. Sharlene and I clung to each other as our poodle skirts flew over our heads.

The train slithered down the track and disappeared around the bend. I stared after it in disbelief. I looked around. A farmer shook his head while he pulled out a handkerchief from his back pocket and wiped his face. A young mother smoothed down her little boy's dishevelled hair. An elderly couple slowly rose from their lawn chairs. The band members began to put away their instruments, shaking their heads. The Stick, in a trance, packed up his radio.

Someone broke the awkward silence with a sharp laugh. Then another broke out in a chuckle. It was contagious. Soon everyone around me laughed.

I glanced over at the principal. He laughed so hard he took off his glasses and wiped his eyes with the back of his hand.

Compiled by Gary Doi

JOHN DIEFENBAKER

Sharlene grinned. "At least we didn't get sucked under the train."

I shuddered. Then I thought about it and laughed too. How funny we must have all looked. Did Mr. Diefenbaker even see us standing there in foolish anticipation?

The farmers returned to their fields, mothers took their children home for lunch, the old folks went to the café for a cup of tea and Sharlene and I, along with the rest of the students and teachers, went back to our classes. At least we had a morning off school and some much-needed excitement. For a long time after, we talked about the event and had a good laugh every time we thought about the day Dief almost came to town.

To his credit, John Diefenbaker sent a note of apology to the mayor, explaining that our town had not been on his itinerary. He did, however, appreciate our support. We all got to see the letter. Just holding a letter written by the prime minister, made me feel special, and full of hope.

Darlene Foster is a writer, employment counsellor, ESL teacher, wife, mother and grandmother. Her grandson calls her "super-mega-woman-supreme". Brought up on a ranch in southern Alberta, she dreamt of travelling the world and meeting interesting people. She lives with her husband on the west coast of BC with their black cat Monkey. Darlene has written three children's travel/adventure books, Amanda in Arabia – The Perfume Flask, Amanda in Spain – The Girl in The Painting, and Amanda in England-The Missing Novel. She believes everyone is capable of making their dreams come true.

THE FIRST SNOW FALL

By Nina Munteanu (Lunenburg, Nova Scotia)

With Christmas nearing, we are reminded of the spirit of generosity and gratitude. I'm Canadian and for me, it always starts with the first snowfall. A few days ago, on the Winter Solstice, a dump of snow covered the Earth in white billows. Huge flakes drifted down from heaven like confetti in a breeze.

We are having a white Christmas. And in Vancouver, BC—usually green and wet at Christmas—it's the first time in over ten years.

I love it.

I love how snow wraps everything in a blanket of soft acceptance. How it creates a dazzling face on a dark Earth. How it refuses to distinguish between artificial and natural. It covers everything—decorated house, shabby old car, willowy trees, manicured lawn—beneath its white mantle. I love how it quiets the Earth.

Have you ever gone for an evening walk in the fresh crisp snow, boots crunching, snow glistening in the moonlight? Each step is its own symphony of textured sound. A kind of collaboration with the deep of the night and Nature's own whisperings.

I grew up in southern Quebec, where the first snow often came from the sky in a thick passion. Huge flakes of unique beauty settled on my coat sleeves and within minutes I was covered in snow. It always saddened me to watch these graceful

Compiled by Gary Doi

shapes melt.

Snow is a shape shifter: charging down in a fierce and mighty blizzard on a chilling wind. Slanting down in a wet sheet, heavy with rain. Quietly spectacular as hoar frost that grows on its surface as water vapor migrates up the snow base on cold, clear nights. Snow is a gypsy, conspiring with the clever wind to form mini-tornadoes and swirling on the cold pavement like misbehaving fairies. It drifts like a vagabond and piles up, cresting over the most impressive structure, creating phantoms out of icons. Some, fearful of the chaos and confusion that snow brings, hide indoors out of the cold. Others embrace its many forms, punching holes through the snow crust to find the treasure of powder beneath or plowing through its softness, leaving behind an ivory trail of adventure.

Snow is magic. It reveals as it cloaks. Animals leave their telltale tracks behind their silent sleuthing. No two snowflakes are alike. Yet every non-aggregated snowflake forms a six-fold radial symmetry, based on the hexagonal alignment of water molecules when they form ice. Tiny perfectly shaped ice-flowers drift down like world peace and settle in a gentle carpet of white. Oddly, a snowflake is really clear and colourless. It only looks white because the whole spectrum of light bounces off the crystal facets in diffuse reflection. My son, who skis, extols "champagne powder"—very smooth and dry snow ideal for gliding on. On powder days, after a fresh snowfall, the mountain trees form glabrous Moore-like sculptures.

Skiers wind their way between the "snow ghosts", leaving meandering "snake-tracks" behind them.

Snow is playful. It beckons you to stick out your tongue and taste the clouds. Snow is like an unruly child. Snow is the trickster. It stirs things up. Makes a mess. It is the herald of change, invigorating, fresh and wondrous. Cars skid in it and squeal with objection. Grumpy drivers honk their horns, impatient to get home; while others sigh in their angry wake. Brown slush flies in a chaotic fit behind a bus and splatters your new coat. Boys (of all ages) venture outside, mischief glinting in their eyes, and throw snowballs. Great battles are fought in backyards where awesome forts are built and defended with fierce determination.

Snow is Christmas. It brings out the best and the worst in people. The Christmas season—whether you are a Christian celebrating the birth of Jesus or of another faith celebrating the season of Joy and Giving—provides each of us with the opportunity to be exactly who we are and who we are meant to be. It is a time

Compiled by Gary Doi

to be genuine. A time to be sincere. A time to be REAL. A time to make the best of our lot and be thankful: whether we are celebrating a turkey feast with a family we don't get along with, spending it alone in a new town, or working the night shift in a busy firm. It is a time to be thankful for the gifts we have been blessed with, even the hardships. Especially the hardships. For they are ours to carry. Ours to make into something wonderful. Like snow.

> **Nina Munteanu** (ninamunteanu.com) has written several novels, short stories, and essays published worldwide and translated into several languages. Nina teaches and coaches writing through her website. Her acclaimed "The Fiction Writer: Get Published, Write Now!" is currently the textbook for creative writing classes at several universities and schools in North America.

Mother's Rebirth

By Sterling Haynes (West Kelowna, British Columbia)

Elizabeth Sterling Haynes (1898 – 1957)

December 7th, 1941 lives on in my memory. Even though I was only fourteen years old at the time, I distinctly remember what happened to my family that day.

It was two o'clock in the afternoon. The Sawatsky twins and my best friend Percy and I were skating at the Garneau Community rink in Edmonton. (Well, sort of skating. We were actually playing a game of tag not condoned by arena officials.) Blaring out over the arena speakers was the song, "I've got a Lovely Bunch of Coconuts". Halfway through, the music stopped and an announcer said, "The United States has declared war on Japan. The American naval and marine casualties at Pearl Harbor are large and many war ships were destroyed." Then the music came back on and everyone it seemed resumed skating.

Soon after, Dad appeared outside the fence of the skating rink. His face was ashen, his lips set tight. I just knew in that moment something was terribly wrong and it wasn't the news of war. It had to be about mother.

"Sterling, change your skates right away. Mother is really sick. You have to transfuse your mother with your blood," he said. "We need at least a quart of blood from you and another quart from Shirley."

At age 43, my mother (Elizabeth Sterling Haynes) had developed cancer of the womb and received preoperative radium inserts to contain her malignancy. A few days earlier, Mother underwent a hysterectomy and lost a significant amount of blood. Surgeon-gynecologist Dr. Horner determined that she was still bleeding and urgently required two massive blood transfusions to save her life.

Dad had taken the car out of the garage and parked on 84th Avenue in front of our house. My sister Shirley was already sitting in the front seat. The tires crunched through snow and ice as Dad drove the four blocks to the University Hospital.

Dr. Horner was waiting at the top steps of the hospital. He rushed us into a small operating room theatre that was divided by a raised six-foot stage. It contained a stretcher, numerous lengths of glass partitions and a long piece of rubber tubing. I climbed the stairs to the raised platform. As I shed my warm clothes and pealed down my long winter underwear, the doctor instructed me to lie on the stretcher. Mother lay pale and motionless on a stretcher below me.

"Dad, is Mom okay? She'll be okay Dr. Horner? Won't she?"

"Yes son, she'll be okay once she gets your blood into her. You pay strict attention to what Dr. Horner tells you," said Dad.

"Sterling, I am going to put a large needle into your arm and we are going to run blood from your arm to your mother's arm," said Dr. Horner. "Your mother is very tired now but as soon as the blood is given she will perk up. The blood will flow by gravity. You must lie still for about an hour, you understand."

"Yes sir, I understand, I won't move a muscle. I'm pretty tough. Hope Mom will be okay soon."

The blood started to flow down the rubber tubing like a massive umbilical cord.

After about an hour Mother seemed a little restless and spoke to me. "Are you alright, Sterling? You know, I feel better already," she said in a low husky voice.

"Yeah, I'm okay Mom. I've got lots of blood. I'm a big strong kid. When I'm finished here Shirley is waiting to come in and give you more blood."

My eyes widened as I looked down at my pale mother. The red life line tubing was prominent against the white sheets and her arm. Mother was sobbing.

Shirley came in and lay on the stretcher where I had been. Dr. Horner disconnected the needle from my arm and hooked the long rubber tubing to a new needle in my sister's arm. I was a bit light-headed at first. Dr. Horner told me I'd given my mother over two pints of blood but I could go back to school the next day.

My dad and sister stayed with Mother at the hospital. Dad told me to walk home and get supper ready and they'd be back around 7:00 pm.

"Your Mom will be fine now. Your Group O, Rh positive blood was a great 44th birthday present to her," said Dr. Horner.

Yes, ironically, December 7th was my mother's birthday.

I remember walking back home along the roadway at dusk. People were putting their house lights on and the bulbs cast a yellow glow to the long shadows. I kicked the large frozen horse droppings left from horse pulled bread wagons and milk carts. I knew Mom would be better now with our new blood and would soon be home from the hospital. I started to sing and dance as I walked along the icy and snow covered road – "*I've got a lovely bunch of coconuts, big ones, thick ones some as big as your head.*"

Mother made a complete recovery from the surgery and lived for another seventeen years. The treatment of radium implants, though, created serious problems ultimately resulting in kidney failure. Yet, in that time period from 1941-1958, Mother was reborn as a teacher, dramatist and writer. She taught drama at the University of Alberta's drama department and Studio Theatre. She inspired student actors and actresses and established "Drama" as an elective subject in the Alberta high school curriculum. Today her legacy to Alberta theatre has been established in perpetuity, by the Sterling Awards given annually to the best actors, playwrights, directors, producers and drama teachers in Alberta.

In 1950, Mother wrote:
"The door of the Studio Theatre opened and a girl came in . . . young and eager, walking as if, already, she saw her name in lights. I had never actually seen that girl before—and yet I had seen her many times, in many hopeful faces. To me she is always Miss Alberta, dreaming of becoming an actress."

Compiled by Gary Doi

University Hospital, Edmonton, Alberta

(Image courtesy of Peel's Prairie Provinces, a digital initiative of the University of Alberta Libraries)

Sterling Haynes may have retired as a medical doctor, but through his stories he is able to share his fascinating experiences practicing medicine in the Cariboo, Alberta and Alabama. His work has been published in such magazines as Okanagan Life, The BC Medical Journal, North of 50, The Medical Post and The Rocky Mountain Goat. In March, 2013, he was presented with the Okanagan Arts Council Literary Arts award. His first book Bloody Practice was a BC bestseller for creative nonfiction and his second book Wake-Up Call is now available as an e-book.

THE WASHING AND THE WINNOWING

By Debra Eve (Los Angeles, California)

What do you see first when you look at this woman?

I notice her smile, then the medal that proclaims her faith, and then, bizarrely, the bar of soap in the foreground. She's a washwoman and those rapids, her washing machine.

It's an intriguing, Life Magazine-worthy portrait, snapped seventy years ago in 1944.

General Douglas MacArthur and the American liberation forces had just landed on her island in the Philippines.

Historians use the term "the human face of war" to remind us what each side in any conflict shares. It mostly refers to soldiers and those actively engaged in the war effort.

They seldom discuss civilians persevering with mundane chores like harvesting and washing and winnowing, or caring for animals and children—small acts of humanity that make meaning from chaos.

I find these photos I share with you poignant on so many levels. They depict people carrying on despite great doubt and hardship. They capture a way of life that has all but vanished—one dependent on cycles and seasons. And finally, they embody the sensitivity of one 20-year-old soldier who would become my father.

My dad was a 5'9", 125-lb professional artist who never should have been drafted. Before World War II, he worked for Disney as an apprentice animator, a career he left

Pounding

Washing

school at age 16 to pursue. He was also an accomplished draughtsman and photographer.

He flunked his U.S. Army physical for being underweight. But they needed his skills, so they shipped him out to the Pacific Theatre with the Signal Photo Corps.

The Corps acted as Xerox copiers before the machine went mainstream—all plans and missives had to be photographed for sharing with headquarters and battalions.

The Corps' orders extended to documenting all facets of the war, but not to detailing the everyday lives of their allies and enemies.

An old Zen saying goes, "Before enlightenment, chop wood and carry water. After enlightenment, chop wood and carry water." Ironically, the same applies to war.

With an artist's eye and an anthropologist's curiosity, my father wandered the Philippine village where he was stationed, capturing small acts of humanity.

In the Philippines, the rice harvest takes place from November to January. MacArthur landed October 20.

Still, the harvest had to go on. The villagers, both men and women, pounded the rice from its husks. The women sifted it in winnowing baskets and set it out to dry.

Small boys still cared for the family's prize possession, the carabao or water buffalo, which provides (to this day) necessary labor to prepare the fields.

The carabao amazed my father. He couldn't fathom the boys' fearlessness with so large a beast.

He once told me a carabao story. The GIs had an overwhelming desire for some "real food" after eating from cans for several weeks before landing.

An enterprising villager learned of the American penchant for "steak and eggs" and hung a sign in his storefront claiming to serve them for a price. The eggs, in fact, were delicious, from local hens.

The "steak," however, was carabao meat, the vilest, toughest stuff my father had ever eaten. The villager must have made a nice profit, considering the value placed on carabao as draft animals.

The Americans, however, paid for their meat craving in more ways than one, since many got upset stomachs!

I'd wish I could tell you that after the war, my father found a rewarding job—that Disney made him a master animator or National Geographic hired him as a photographer.

But as the war dragged on, he became mired in documenting

Caraballa

Fly Like an Eagle — Real Life Stories of Hope and Inspiration

Winnowing

Debra Eve is a proud late bloomer and possessor of many passions. At 36, she became an archaeologist. At 42, a martial arts instructor. At 46, she married the love of her life. Now she writes about fellow late bloomers while plotting her next grand adventure. Her inspiring profiles can be found at LaterBloomer.com. Debra received her M.A. in Anthropology from UCLA, where she was the last research assistant to archaeomythologist Marija Gimbutas, a colleague of Joseph Campbell. She helped bring Dr. Gimbutas' final book, The Living Goddesses, to print.

battles and atrocities. He never really recovered from it.

Disney didn't rehire him, and without a high school diploma, he found getting work difficult.

He did stints as a camera salesman for Sears, a draughtsman for a machining catalog, and a photo finisher for a Kodak franchise. His post-traumatic stress worsened. But he couldn't talk about it or get help, since the condition was only named and recognized after Viet Nam.

He died twenty years ago, a broken man, from the side effects of alcoholism.

Right before he passed away, he gave me his fifty-year-old cardboard box of World War II photos and urged, "Do something with them. For history. So we don't forget."

And I did. I majored in anthropology and wrote a senior paper on continuity in Philippine subsistence farming methods.

I scanned my dad's photos, restored some, and posted them to an archival web site, "The Pacific War Photos of Pfc Glenn W. Eve".

Not long ago, Oxford University Press contacted me for permission to use one in *The Oxford Illustrated History of the Second World War,* due out next year. So my father will get his Life Magazine moment after all.

I wish Oxford had chosen the smiling washwoman with the testament to faith around her neck.

I believe she's as worthy of inclusion as Roosevelt or Churchill. Her message is as moving.

Every time I look at her, I notice something new—how long and elegant her fingers, how ingeniously she's turned a skirt into a sundress, how genuine her smile, not at all posed (but of course, it must have been). The hallmark of a great photographer and an equally remarkable subject.

How old is she? Twenty, the same age as my father at the time? Could she still be alive?

And I sigh.

Oxford didn't want her. They wanted a photo of Manila's devastation.

A few years ago, in response to this emphasis on tragedy, I started a blog that profiles late-blooming artists and writers—those whose lives have been touched by hardship, but who overcame it to produce timeless and self-healing works of art. I wish my father could have been one.

Still, these images survive in all their humanity, both my dad's and those he photographed, a reminder that war is the great equalizer.

A reminder that in times of doubt and tragedy, the bravest thing we can do is take care of the children and the washing and the winnowing.

Compiled by Gary Doi

The Best

By Cathryn Wellner (Kelowna, British Columbia)

Richard and I had talked about marriage during our months together, but we had both been down that road before and were in no hurry. As time rolled by, my being American made my stay on Vancouver Island tenuous. Still, we tiptoed around the idea of formalizing our relationship.

We had begun performing a combination of music and storytelling. Audiences seemed to enjoy one of our programs in particular, "Partners for the Long Dance," a wry, poignant look at relationships through stories and song. One of the songs we often sang for it was "Dear Old Buffalo Boy," a back-and-forth, musical conversation between a man and a woman who are planning a wedding until she finds out he already has six children.

In the version we sang, the woman asks, "When will we be married?"

He replies, "I guess we'll get married in a week."

One night at the Cowichan Folk Guild, Richard changed the words. When I sang, "When will we be married," Richard didn't miss a beat.

"How about June 29th?" he said.

Richard figured everyone would laugh, but the audience had been watching us for months. Instead of laughing, they were speculating.

I was flustered. Richard filled the long pause with chords on his autoharp, then we picked up the song and went on.

When we got home later, we looked at the calendar. June 29th was a Saturday, and we had no plans. So we called Pine Lodge Farm and booked the whole place for a wedding.

Richard was a little nervous about telling his sons. He figured Raven, his younger son, would be pleased but was less sure of Richard Jr., who was more conservative and cautious. As it turned out, both gave their blessings.

He didn't tell me he had talked with his oldest son. One day I said to him at dinner, "You'd better call Rich and tell him we're going to be in Vancouver on Sunday." The plan was to tell the family in person. That meant Richard's two sons, his two brothers, his sister-in-law, his father and his father's partner.

Richard picked up the phone, talked with Rich briefly, then handed the phone to me and said, "Here. You can tell him."

I should have known he would not have left me to convey the message. Still, I was about to settle into a glare when young Richard said, "Congratulations."

I had to laugh. That is the way it is with second marriages. The parents' reactions are not the critical ones. It is the children's blessings that count.

Neither of us had any religious affiliation, but Richard knew of a minister who was new in town. He had asked me to interview her for the local paper. I liked her from the first question. She was warm and open and not in the least dogmatic. When I later showed her the piece I had written about her, she burst into tears...the happy kind. We

Fly Like an Eagle — Real Life Stories of Hope and Inspiration

Wedding *Ever*

figured she was just the ticket to tie the knot on a second marriage.

After we told our families and secured a minister, we began compiling a list and sending out invitations for our June wedding. In my year in Duncan, Richard's friends had made me feel welcome. They were on the list along with friends from both our pasts.

Since we were involved in creative pursuits, our guest list included writers, storytellers, musicians, poets, photographers and artists. As acceptances flowed in, we were sure we were planning the most interesting wedding either of us had ever attended. The rooms in Pine Lodge filled quickly. Nearby motels accommodated others. Guests came from as far east as New York, as far south as California and as close as the town we were living in.

Unlike newlyweds, we did not need pots and pans and towels. Instead, we asked family and friends to bring us their hearts, and, oh, they did. On the day of the wedding, we looked around at so many beloved faces and felt the warm embrace of our scattered community.

Among those who shared their creative souls were Magical Strings, the immensely talented duo of Phil and Pam Boulding. I had performed stories with them from time to time, and we had become good friends. Vi Hilbert agreed to give us a Lushootseed blessing. She was a beloved storyteller and a revered elder of the Upper Skagit tribe. She had adopted me as her granddaughter years before and now took Richard into her extended family of grandchildren. So many talented people joined us, each adding something unique to the mix.

The only glitch was that the wedding nearly happened without me. Vi gave her blessing in Lushootseed and English. The minister welcomed the gathering and then launched into the ceremony. I was still upstairs, waiting for the signal to make my grand entrance. The startled groom stopped the proceedings and sent word to bring down the bride.

Compiled by Gary Doi

When the ceremony ended, the party began. Richard, Jr. was master of ceremonies. Our friends and family had prepared speeches, stories, songs and poems. The only video camera was in our minds, recording the laughter, the tears, the sighs, and the applause. It was the best wedding I have ever been to, and it was mine.

With so many guests from out of town, we hosted a pancake breakfast the next morning. Auchinachie Farm, still new to us, declared itself as a gathering place, a place where all were welcome, where storytelling and music would ring from the rafters and across the fields.

When the last hugs were hugged, the last happy tears shed, the last goodbyes waved, we settled in to figure out what we would do next. Life seemed full of promise. The dreams were bigger than our resources, but in the years we lived on that little farm, we gathered more stories for our rocking-chair years than many people do in a lifetime.

Cathryn Wellner's meandering career path (thisgivesmehope.com; catchingcourage.com) has included stints as a French teacher, a school librarian, an itinerant storyteller, a university instructor, an arts organizer, a community developer, a communications consultant, a farmer and rancher, and a project manager. She is a citizen of two countries and has lived in five. The upside of all that change is stories. Now she has settled down to write them.

RICHARD WRIGHT & CATHRYN WELLNER WEDDING (1991)

Why San Francisco Stole my Heart

By Zee Gorman (San Francisco, California)

Sixty years ago, Tony Bennett sang this famous tune: "I left my heart in San Francisco; high on a hill, it calls to me." He sang about the golden sun, the fog, and the cable cars. In 1993, I took a vacation to San Francisco and never left. I fell in love with this magical city for the same reasons. Having lived and worked in the Bay Area for the past twenty years, I have only found even more reasons for my love.

The day I came into the City for a tech conference pulls it all together.

We disembarked the Golden Gate Ferry at Pier One at 7 a.m. I followed a large crowd onto the street. All traffic paused as we poured into the crosswalks of Embarcadero. I looked around. One, two, three, four, five . . . the crowd was at least eight-person wide and a-minute long. Men, women, young, old, in suits, in ripped jeans, in leather jackets, with black hair, or blonde, red, grey. . . and carrying briefcases, purses, shoulder bags, or backpacks. We cut through an oasis of palm trees, giant water fountains and colorful park benches and dissolved into the high rises of the Financial District.

As I reached the sidewalk of Market Street, the sun was just rising over the bay. In an instant, the top of every object, from trees to buildings, was dyed a glorious orange. I took out my phone and snapped a few timely shots.

Suddenly a gruff voice said in front of me: "Take a picture of me!"

I lowered my phone. And there in front of me was an old man with a weathered face and long grey hair. He wore an old coat gleaming with filth and pushed a shopping cart

Photo credits in this article: Francisco Little (Beijing, China)

full of junk. A homeless man.

I took a few shots of him as he smiled broadly, showing his missing teeth.

"How do I get the pictures to you?" I asked.

"They are for you!" he said.

I thanked him and went on my way, chuckling to myself, "Only in San Francisco would a homeless man stop a business woman to get his picture taken." Then it dawned on me why: This is a City of Compassion.

Project Homeless Connect, a volunteer program organized by the employees of the city government, brings people from all walks to offer services to the homeless. Once a year, the Bill Graham Auditorium opens up to receive thousands of homeless men and women. The services range from a lunch, a bag of groceries, to legal counseling, job assistance, and dentures.

Last year I joined the other volunteers for this memorable experience. The program started with a performance by SOS—Singers of the Street, composed of those affected by homelessness. They sang with such joy and liveliness that I was touched to tears. Later our group went to the cafeteria where we ushered our guests to the tables, took their orders, and served them a nice warm lunch. Then we listened to their stories. . . . We served hundreds upon hundreds. It was a day of learning and celebration. I witnessed how this one-day event not only gives care but also gives hope to those who are less fortunate.

And nothing is more rewarding than being able to give another human being hope.

I watched the retreating back of the old homeless man and reflected upon our exchange. Together with the rising sun, he made my day, before the day even started.

Minutes later I reached my first destination: The Landmark @ One Market. It is a mesh of the historical facet of Southern Pacific Building, built in 1916, with two modern office towers. Salesforce.com, named #1 of the world's most innovative companies by Forbes in both 2012 and 2013, is headquartered here. The 11th floor, which President Obama visited to get a glimpse of how the company's technology helped him get in touch with thousands of voters personally in the 2012 campaign, is a live show of the internet in action. Walls and columns have been turned into giant screens and corridors a theater with a panoramic view. I sent a tweet with a particular keyword and moments later my twitter profile flashed on the screens. This technology allows companies and politicians alike to dialogue directly with their customers and voters based on an instant and automatic analysis of their social media chatters.

There I met with an architect behind the modern magic of Salesforce's "cloud-based computing". He is a patent-holder of over half a dozen inventions. "It's not really work; it's just the power to charm", says his LinkedIn profile. With what? "The Army of Darkness, one of the many things I feel needs to be built." "What is the Army of Darkness?" He went on to explain this highly complex Artificial Intelligence that commands "the cloud" to release computing power at literally a single press of a key - something he felt needs to be built, went on to build it, and once completed would "sell it" to his company. "If I deliver, they'll love me forever." A few weeks later, I received a single-word text from him, "Delivered." I smiled. I knew it was no easy feat for him—between waking

Compiled by Gary Doi

up at 4:30 am to work out before walking to his office for a long day on weekdays and taking his 8-year-old daughter out to do things like visiting the Academy of Science on weekends. Yet his youthful face shows no trace of hard work.

Indeed "it's not really work". It's passion; it's love; it's the daring spirit to conquer the impossible. It's the raw human drive to ever evolve. There are thousands of tech workers just like him in this City of Innovation. A bit down the street from Landmark @ One Market is the new headquarter of Twitter. And then the list just goes on: Instagram, Dropbox, Pinterest, Yelp, and not far down Interstate 101, Oracle, Google, Genentech, Facebook, . . .

The vibes of innovation go beyond technology and tech companies, as a young woman enlightened me on that day. She is San Francisco City's Deputy Innovation Officer and a post-doctorate of Stanford. At the conference, she talked about the City's innovative ideas to improve the life of the citizens in blighted neighborhoods. Some of the ideas are as simple as making government transparent and getting everybody together to talk. ImproveSF, an online forum that connects civil challenges with the communities shows how mere human connection can change lives: People chatter, debate, and the right civil projects get funded and done.

In the afternoon I took a break and strolled down Market Street to Civic Center where historical buildings such as the City Hall, the War Memorial, and the Main Library huddle around a green park. I found dozens of tents had been erected around the street corner. It was the Heart of the City Farmer's Market Day! I used to work near Civic Center and came here every Wednesday to pick up fresh vegetables. Filled with nostalgia, I happily joined the crowd that checked the stalls for their favorite items of fresh produce. I visited every booth and admired the huge selection of flowers, roasted nuts, cheeses, berries and citruses, bread, and juices, . . . and I noticed how every customer there looked relaxed and happy.

No wonder San Francisco is rated as the #4 healthiest city in the U.S. If you live here, you can't help it. There are farmers markets around the city all week long and organic food markets in every district. It never ceases to amaze me as to how this headquarter of technology giants on the one hand takes the world to the future, and on the other, clings on to the root of where we come from: Mother Earth.

Among the farmers I spotted a familiar face—a Chinese woman who sold ethnic Chinese vegetables. It must have been ten years since I had changed jobs and last bought vegetables from her. But we greeted each other warmly and began to catch up in Mandarin. For a moment I felt I was back in my birthplace in China!

Walking back to the conference, I was thankful to have experienced a piece of home and I knew thousands of others from different ethnic backgrounds too, can have a piece of their homes living in this city, by simply visiting farmers markets, ethnic restaurants and groceries stores, and even ethnic department stores.

When evening arrived, I went up to the Views Lounge on the 39th floor of the San Francisco Marriott Marquis. With a glass of wine from a local winery in hand and looking out of the windows at the majestic cityscape, I reflected on the day's encounters.

I realized what makes this city great is the people—who give their heart out to create every new day, to give care, and to connect with each other.

Zee Gorman (zeegorman.blogspot.ca), born in South China during the Cultural Revolution (both her parents were exiled to the countryside for being 'intellectuals'), was raised within layers of political and cultural confines. Yet her love for literature gave wings to a life that would be completely different from that of her parents. She has written short stories, poems, and essays, and is mildly published in China. Her quest and thirst for more understanding of the Western cultures eventually led to her migration to the United States where she completed two Master's Degrees at Northern Arizona University. Today, Zee Gorman lives in Northern California with her husband and her daughter. By night she is a writer, an artist, a crafter... whatever she imagines herself to be and by day she has a career in IT management.

The Being There

By John McLaughlin
(Bathurst, New Brunswick)

Compiled by Gary Doi

As I nestle into the calm of midlife, I am grateful that I have few regrets. What good fortune I've had, I tell myself, to be a citizen of this greatest of countries, and to reap its many blessings. I'm from a family of five baby boom kids, raised by loving parents who modelled kindness, empathy, self-direction and duty. My wife and I chose to settle in our home town, the beautiful coastal City of Bathurst, New Brunswick, where we enjoy the comforts of a close knit community, where friends and neighbors step up for each other in times of need, where our children were embraced with the same values that were passed on to us when we were young.

I love my country, and I love our freedom.

And therein resides one chafing regret that endures and grows across time: as a war veteran's son, I so wish I had made the time to return with my father to the hellish battlefields he endured as a young man (a boy, really) in 1940s Europe. He was a mighty Canadian soldier who, at just 17 years of age, eagerly enlisted with the Royal Regiment of Canada before sailing to Europe to serve his country. He survived the horrific bloodletting at Dieppe, and returned to the European continent at DDay+2, contributing to the perilous Allied push through France, Belgium and into Holland where he was critically wounded on a dark Friday the 13th in October, 1944.

(PICTURE ON THE LEFT:
PRIVATE PATRICK MCLAUGHLIN)

Dieppe.
Falaise.
Hougerheide.

These places appear and reappear, ghostlike and vague, in the dark spaces of my imagination. I've heard them mentioned many times since my youth, have imagined my father's staggering courage as he confronted the reality of war in these places.

His courage, and his fear.

And his horror.

And his grief.

My father passed away six years ago, and I remember the sight of him resting at the funeral home, dressed in his blue blazer set off with a row of bright medals that acknowledged his heroism. His medals, and two little golden bars sewn into the sleeve of his jacket—his wound stripes, one for the shrapnel in his heart and lung, and the other for the missing piece of his right hand. That's when I began to regret. I'd never walk the beach at Dieppe with him. Never see the impossible cliffs that were supposed to be scaled. Never experience with him the simple being-there of European towns he helped to liberate, of streets he made safe, of fields and forests returned to peaceful ways. Never visit with him the resting places of his friends, and weep with him there, as I'm sure we'd have done.

Some years ago, when Dad was still with us, I did, in fact, visit the little town of Hougerheide in Holland, the place where he was shot by an enemy sniper, and where he lay near death (alive only through the miracle of a well-placed notebook crammed with army documents and family snapshots, and a fountain pen carried in his breast pocket that deflected the bullet intended for his heart). I went there twice, actually, once with my daughter and once with my wife. I expected to find a heaviness there, perhaps a more ghastly, vivid representation of the vague imaginings I'd carried with me all these years.

But there was nothing dark for me there. Nothing morbid or frightening or sad.

Only life.

And community.

And shoppers on the main street.

And farmers in the countryside.

And teenagers with cell phones and ear buds and piercings and wild hair-dos.

It struck me that embedded in all of this, this pleasant community existence, was my father's gift to this town: life, happiness, choice.

That's what caused me to well up with emotion. Not sadness, but pride. Not images of fear and loss and horror and grief, but rather the tangible evidence of a country—a continent—blessed with freedom because of the bravery of a Canadian soldier and thousands of others just like him.

My father lived his life after the war tormented by horrible, relentless memories of a time nobody should ever have to endure. At the same time, he was a survivor, and in partnership with our dear mother, he managed to rise above the lingering trauma of war to provide a stable, safe, loving and nurturing home for his family. With everything I've learned about post-traumatic stress in recent years, I don't know how he did it. To be perfectly honest, I don't know how he did any of this.

War is a terrible thing he used to say, and though we rarely discussed it further, I know that in those words lies a horrible truth about things one is forced to do in such a messed-up world. When I think about him, and his service as a Canadian soldier, I wish he had been able to live without regrets, but I know that is not the case. How could it have been when one as good and kind and gentle a man as was one Pte. Patrick E. McLaughlin (from the lovely little Maritime community of Bathurst) marches off to hell and emerges a hero, albeit a scarred and oh-so-wounded one.

So what of my regret? It is comforting, I suppose, to realize that through my father's sacrifices, I am able to enjoy this fairly perfect life in a very free society, where such regrets are about as bad as it gets. Some day I'll visit Dieppe and Falaise, and I'll return to Hougerheide, without my father, of course, but knowing that he is there. The being there is possible.

His gift endures.

John McLaughlin is Deputy Minister at the New Brunswick Department of Education & Early Childhood Development. As a former teacher and superintendent of schools, he believes the education system should nurture a sense of goodness in students, so they graduate from high school equipped not just with strong academic skills, but also with a desire to contribute positively to the world and to care for its people. John and his wife, Cathy, have four grown daughters, and they live in Bathurst on New Brunswick's beautiful northeastern coast.

Compiled by Gary Doi

Memory & Mystery
Meaning & Magic

Two elderly ladies were enjoying the sunshine on a park bench. They had been meeting at the same park every sunny day for over 12 years . . . chatting, and enjoying each other's company.

One day, the younger of the two ladies, turns to the other and says, "Please don't be angry with me, but I am embarrassed, after all these years, my memory is not what it used to be... What is your name? I just can't remember."

The older friend stares at her, looking very confused, says nothing for a while and finally says, "How soon do you need to know?"

Memory can be a frustrating thing. We remember things we wish we didn't, and forget things we wish we remembered. It all feels a little out of your control. In the classic novel A Prayer for Owen Meany, John Irving writes,

"Your memory is a monster; you forget—it doesn't. It simply files things away. It keeps things for you, or hides things from you—and summons them to your recall with will of its own. You think you have a memory; but it has you!"

This is mostly true, although we can control the focus of memory to a certain extent. It's a beautiful thing if you can draw inspiration from the positive memories and find some healing and transformation in the difficult memories.

MEMORY AND GRATITUDE

We can't control memory, but we have more power than we often imagine. By focusing on gratitude, it's amazing how motivating memories start to fill your mind space.

Memory is one of the basic ingredients of gratitude, which is in turn one of the basic ingredients of optimism. When I'm at funerals, listening to eulogies, it often strikes me that it would be SO powerful to tell each other's stories like this while we are still alive. Imagine the gratitude if we took every opportunity to share memories and each other's positive attributes while we are still around to hear it.

There is a funny story about a minister who is leading a memorial service. He calls on people to come forward and say a few nice words about the deceased. No one comes forward. He urges them, "Surely someone present today can say something appreciative!" Eventually a man comes to the microphone and says, "His brother was worse."

In most cases, this is not a problem. Once someone has gone, memories come to us of good times shared and admirable qualities. They comfort and inspire us. These memories often lead to forgiveness and healing.

Fly Like an Eagle — Real Life Stories of Hope and Inspiration

By Ian Lawton
(Grand Haven, Michigan)

Memory and Perspective

Gutzon Borglum, the sculptor who created the amazing Mount Rushmore Memorial, was once asked if he considered his work perfect in detail. "Not yet," he replied. "The nose of Washington is an inch too long. It's better that way, though. It'll erode to be approximately right in about 10,000 years."

Memory tends to be like that. We erode the imperfections of the past into a coherent whole, integrate even the difficult memories, and move forward. In time, memories fall into place as they need to.

Fill your memories with a lot of acceptance, and forgiveness. Everything was the way it was then, and now you have the power of perspective. You see more, you know more. Everything is unfolding at it needs to, including the evolving story your memory is telling.

Compiled by Gary Doi

Photo credit: Gary Doi

MEMORY AND CHANGE

We all have stories and a lineage. Our memories are built on these stories that are part fact and part fiction. It's not so much that we retrieve memories. We reweave memories in a way that feels consistent. Many of our rituals and traditions are built on these memories. There is an old Jewish story that makes this point.

When the great Rabbi Israel Baal Shem-Tov felt anxious about the future, he went to a special place in the forest to meditate. He would light the fire, say a special prayer, and sure enough his anxiety would subside. Sometimes, amazing things would happen after his forest ritual. Years later when he was gone, it fell to the next generation to deal with the same anxiety. The head Rabbi knew the story of his ancestor in the forest but didn't know all the details. He knew where to go in the forest and even knew the words of the prayer, but didn't remember how to light the fire. So he would go to the same place in the forest and say: "I do not know how to light the fire, but I am still able to say the prayer," and sure enough his anxiety would subside. Another generation later, the same ritual would take place but with even less memory of the detail. The Rabbi would go into the forest and say, "I do not know how to light the fire. I do not remember the prayer, but I know the place and this must be sufficient." It was always enough. The years passed. Finally the next generation the head Rabbi only had a very small knowledge of the ritual. Sitting in his armchair, his head in his hands, he said: "I am unable to light the fire, and I do not remember the prayer. I cannot even find the place in the forest. All I can do is tell the story, and this must be sufficient." Telling the stories from the past, with the mingling of fact and fiction, is important.

Ritual and memory are like that. When I was growing up, our family had a Christmas ritual that we inherited from an English custom. Christmas pudding, steamed and served with brandy butter and cream. The earlier custom was to include certain items in the pudding before cooking it; silver coins for wealth, tiny wishbones for good luck, a ring for marriage etc. Whoever found the items in their pudding on Christmas day would get what they chomped on. When I was young, my parents would put coins in the pudding that they had collected from their parents; shillings and sixpence and the like. The coins must have gone missing, because by the time I was about 10 they were using current day coins. Then when people started losing teeth on their Christmas pudding, we stopped putting coins in the pudding altogether. But we still ate the pudding and brandy butter endures to this day. Just like the story of the Rabbis, eating the pudding and telling stories about the coins of Christmas past was always enough.

Tradition, ritual and memory are based on an ever changing story. As Nancy Jordan said,

"No sooner did I bend over and scratch the soil with the hoe than I began to unearth bits and pieces of my past. Memories forever rooted in time were clustered in my garden consciousness like potatoes, waiting, crying to be dug up. I plant flowers and vegetables. I harvest memories – and life."

MEMORY AND NATURE

Nature has always been the focus of significant memories both for individuals and cultures. The ancient story is told that while the Hebrew people were in exile, they were desperate and anxious. The rainbow was their reminder that they were part of something larger than their circumstance. Before they understood how rainbows came about, they no doubt filled it with supernatural meaning. The rainbow reminded them to look for hope beyond any natural disaster like a flood and larger than their exile. They were comforted by the evolving reality that all things are constantly moving and changing. Despair and grief may feel like the last word, but there is always a rainbow close by the rain. Rainbows are universally loved, even now that we do understand how they occur. The meaning we place on rainbows, however, might be different.

I remember taking a wedding on a beach a few years back. Clouds were looming and the bride was getting anxious. People were constantly looking up at the sky to check for rain. A few drops of rain began to fall, smudging the marriage license. Just when we were about to turn and run for cover, the rain stopped and a massive rainbow appeared right above us. The timing couldn't have been more perfect. It was as if the rainbow was framing the happy couple like a gazebo. The rainbow was a reminder not to give up.

There is always more to come. There is always more to learn, more to understand and more to come. We now know that there is nothing supernatural about a rainbow. It's all about the refraction of light as it passes through water. There is nothing supernatural, but there is something magical about the rainbow. It's AS IF the rainbow is coming from beyond. It's the same with memories and ritual. There is nothing supernatural about memories that appear to come from nowhere. They are stored in the brain, even if you don't realize it. Carl Jung described the personal unconscious as: "lost memories, painful ideas that are repressed, subliminal perceptions... and contents that are not yet ripe for consciousness."

It's all stored somewhere in the brain. It's not supernatural but there is something magical about the healing qualities of recovered memories that can turn wounds into wisdom and pain into perspective.

Do you ever arrive somewhere for the first time and "feel" like you've been there before? Maybe it's a smell or a sound that triggers your memory of another time or place. The memory could trigger a protective instinct or some kind of reassurance. For me, the smell of pine after rain in the woods triggers an incredible surge of optimism. A 20 minute walk in the woods takes me back to childhood hikes. The smell of the beach refuels me. There is a sign at our local beach that says, "No refueling on the beach." I always smile at the sign because this is one of the places where I totally refuel. The beach takes me back to childhood vacations, hours lying on the sand before we knew about the dangers of sun exposure. In our blissful ignorance, we would spend hours refueling each summer.

Nature, in all its beauty, is a playground for the senses and a memory emporium. It's a place to be inspired by happy memories and heal difficult memories.

MEMORY AND MYSTERY

Memory remains one of the great mysteries of consciousness. How do birds travel thousands of miles and apparently stop at the same points each year on their trek? How do they know? How do new generations of birds know to continue the same route? Are they taking visual cues or following their nose? No one knows for sure. Then there is the clownfish; remember, Nemo? After clownfish hatch from their eggs, they spend 10 to 12 days in the open sea, carried out by currents. But they often miraculously find their way back to the reefs where they were born. Apparently they sniff for leaves that fall into the sea from rainforests near their coral reef homes. Memory fills their senses and brings them home.

Do you have moments of déjà vu and wonder where in your memory the experience is coming from? Do you sometimes say something and wonder where your information came from? Memory is a mystery to be mined for meaning.

Part of the beauty of imagination is when we have memories of the future, and understand with confidence what needs to be said or done. As the White Queen says to Alice in Through the Looking Glass, "It's a poor sort of memory that only works backwards." The Queen warns her that having memories that go both ways can make you giddy at first.

Maybe the point where memories collide in both directions is dreams. Dreams seem to be the brain's way of consolidating memories. Dreams are a complex and confusing combination of memories, maybe a clearing house, where you put unlikely people in the same situation and play out frightening and delightful scenarios.

Memories are personal, subjective and evolving. As Philip Roth wrote,

"Each of us remembers and forgets in a pattern whose labyrinthine windings are an identification mark no less distinctive than a fingerprint."

Dreams and memories connect you with hidden powers. Deep down you have a memory of who you are at your essence, an essence that the anxieties and traumas of life have partially robbed from your conscious mind. Explore your dreams, memories and surprising thoughts to recover some of the power of your full humanity. Once you recover some of this essence, you will feel liberated to live through floods and see the rainbows, for there is always more to come, more to learn and more to REMEMBER. Remember the two small words in the middle of remember; ME and BE. There is more ME to BE.

Ian Lawton (soulseeds.com) is a spiritual leader of a growing worldwide community with a 20 year background in pastoral, change and grief support. He is an author and lectures internationally on contemporary spirituality. He has been blogging and writing daily affirmations for several years. Ian and his wife Meg are the founders of Soulseeds – a site designed to help make people's lives and this world a thriving garden.

Compiled by Gary Doi

Far, far away,
There's a mountain, as high up as the clouds.
In the mountain there's a temple,
and in the temple there's a bell.

The bell strikes noon and midnight
On its own
Everyday
For hundreds of years.

Then one day, it stops.

Birds, monkeys, squirrels . . .
They all come to ask:
Why have you stopped, bell?

The bell says:
I've followed the temple all my life.
When the temple is in the sunlight of the noon,

Why have you stopped facing the sun and the moon?
The mountain says:
I have followed the cloud all my life.
It comes and goes,
but now it has stopped moving.

Everyone goes to ask the cloud:
What is your deal?
Why have you stopped spinning?

The cloud says for hundreds of years
I have followed the water.
The water flows and it washes over the rock,
And the rock comes and goes.
That tells me when to move.
But the water has stopped.

Everyone goes to the water
And demands an answer as to why it has stopped flowing.

Holiday Musings

I strike;
When the temple is in the moonlight of the midnight,
I strike.
But the temple is now doing nothing, so I stop.

Everyone asks the temple:
Why are you not in the sunlight or the moonlight?

The temple says:
I have followed the mountain all my life.
It spins and spins
So I can be facing the sun and the moon.
But it has stopped spinning
So I don't know what to do.

Everyone goes to ask the mountain:

The water says:
I don't know. I'm just following the rock.
When the rock moves, I move.

Of course now everyone goes to the rock and demands
an answer.

The rock says:
I'm just taking a break.
. . .
Whoever you are that makes the world go round,
I hope you have a nice break.

Love --
The water, the cloud, the temple, the mountain, the bell, the
birds, the squirrels, the monkeys, and everyone.

By Zee Gorman (San Francisco, California)

Early Morning Workout in Shanghai

- Francisco Little, Photographer (Beijing, China)

33

Compiled by Gary Doi

Herding Instinct

- Gary Doi, Photographer (British Columbia, Canada)

Bringing it Home

By Sarah Dahlen (Monterey Bay, California)

Carlos Ramos loves to read the stories and legends of his country, but he has never checked out a library book. Like most Guatemalan children, this fourth grader has not had access to a lending library. Books are expensive and hard to come by in Guatemala, and libraries, which are much less common than in North America, are reluctant to circulate books because of their inability to replace those that may be damaged or not returned at all.

This scarcity of books means that even Guatemalan families with some disposable income are unlikely to have many books at home. Carlos and his older brother, who live with their grandmother in Quetzaltenango (Xela) while their mother works in the capital to support the family, only have a chance

Fly Like an Eagle – Real Life Stories of Hope and Inspiration

to read for pleasure when their classes visit the school library, maybe once or twice a week.

Carlos wants to be a portrait artist when he grows up, and he knows that he will have to study hard to achieve his goal. With limited access to books, however, he is unable to fully reap the benefits of recreational reading, which are many. Reading for pleasure has been linked not only to improved reading comprehension, but also to improved writing skills, vocabulary, spelling, and grammar. It corresponds with improved academic achievement, increased participation in civic and cultural events, and an inclination for lifelong learning. Developing a culture of reading would be a significant benefit to Guatemala, a country whose literacy rate of 76% is the lowest in Central America.

But as long as Carlos and his peers have limited access to books, the creation of a culture of reading seems out of reach.

Carlos has an advantage over many 9-year-olds in Guatemala, however, in that he attends the Miguel Angel Asturias Academy, a non-profit K-12 school in Xela, Guatemala's second largest city. The school's director, Jorge Chojolán, is an educational visionary who, in the face of many bureaucratic obstacles, has created a school founded on principles of social justice. Students at Asturias Academy focus their studies around relevant monthly themes, including racism, gender equity, and environmental sustainability.

When asked if there is anything about his country he hopes will change, Carlos said, "I don't like the litter everywhere." This issue may be on his mind because, in honor of Earth Day, April's theme at Asturias Academy is ecology and environmental sustainability. Carlos and his classmates learn about local flora and fauna and how to take care of their shared environment. Carlos hopes that the environmental situation in his country can improve, and has some concrete suggestions: no littering, no burning tires, and no cutting down trees.

The Asturias Academy Library does its best to carry books related to ecology and the school's other monthly themes, but with a limited budget they rely heavily on book donations from foreign organizations. One such organization is Librarians Without Borders (LWB), a non-profit founded in 2005 by librarians hoping to rectify some of the disparities in access to books and information among different areas of the world. A small, volunteer-run organization, LWB has been working with Asturias Academy since 2009. In that time, they have assisted in identifying the needs of the library and creating sustainable solutions to meet those needs.

The sustainability of library solutions is a critical component of the LWB work, as the intention is for the Asturias Library, or any other library partnering with the organization, to not be dependent on foreign aid for their ongoing operations. LWB has provided support, through some combination of planning, funding, and implementation, with the physical design of the Asturias Library, the development of the collection, the classification and organization of the books, the creation of an inventory and catalog, and the provision of library-related programs to students. The next border to be crossed is circulation.

Circulation, for those outside of the library world, refers to the system and process that allow libraries to lend books to their patrons. In a country where children do not have much exposure to books and often lack the accompanying understanding of their treatment and respect for their value, libraries' fears about the loss and damage of books that could result from lending are understandable. Nonetheless, Asturias Academy, recognizing its potential role in contributing to a culture of reading in Guatemala, has decided to circulate its books to students.

The announcement to students that they would soon be able to take books home with them was made in April 2013 during a service trip of Librarians Without Borders to Asturias Academy. The organization had been asked to provide instruction for students that would increase their awareness of both the benefits and the responsibilities that accompany borrowing library books. Librarians, engaging the students with skits and games, covered the steps for selecting and checking out a book, taking care of it at home, and bringing it back the next day. When students learned that they would soon be able to put these steps into practice, they were overjoyed, with spontaneous applause and fist bumps erupting from the enthusiastic group.

There was instruction, there was excitement, and then...a pause. As is understandably the case in libraries or schools that have a number of competing priorities and insufficient staff and funding, the lending of books was pushed back and delayed until, one year later, the promise to students had not yet been fulfilled. LWB, conscious of their role as supporters rather than drivers of the process, returned to Asturias Academy once again to see how they could help.

It appeared that, as much as anything, moral support was what was needed. The organization was able to create a simplified circulation system to track the library's lending and give a refresher session on checking out books to the sixth grade class, which had been selected to pilot the process. On April 23, 2014, giddy sixth graders handed over their library cards in exchange for books to take home for the evening. All books were returned

Compiled by Gary Doi

(Photo credit: Carmen Ho)

in good condition the following morning, and the school plans to move forward with the pilot, lending to one class each week. Eventually, the Asturias library aims to expand its impact even further, lending books to the families of students and to the community.

As for Carlos, he did not yet know when the fourth grade class would take its turn bringing home books to read, but he knew what he might want to check out first: a book of Guatemalan legends.

(Photo credit: Sarah Dahlen)

Sarah Dahlen is a Reference and Instruction Librarian at California State University, Monterey Bay. She is the treasurer of REFORMA, the national organization to promote library and information services to Latinos and Spanish speakers, and has traveled to Guatemala twice with Librarians without Borders.

Rescuing a Red-tailed Hawk

By Dave Whitton (Summerland, British Columbia)

Sometimes, a happenstance encounter with Mother Nature can create something truly wonderful. Such was the case with Denis and Gerry Marson, a retired couple from Coldstream, British Columbia.

One afternoon in early spring 2012, Denis and Gerry noticed two red-tailed hawks soaring in wide circles high in the sky. The large, stocky bird with its distinctive markings, brown with a white breast and a rust-colored tail, was not an uncommon sighting in the area. Yet it was the birds' behavior which drew their attention. Denis and Gerry watched in amazement as the birds performed a courtship "dance" in the sky. One of the hawks dove steeply, then shot up again at an angle nearly as steep, then approached the other bird from above with extended legs. The pair then clasped talons and plummeted in spirals toward the ground before pulling away.

The very next day, they saw the hawks refurbishing a nest in the crown of a tall fir tree. Denis and Gerry had the perfect vantage point from the sunroom in their house. They could observe all the goings-on.

Weeks went by, and it soon became obvious the hawks were incubating eggs. During the nestling stage, the parents took turns flying off to hunt and returning to feed the new born chicks. As the baby birds grew bigger so did their appetites, and the feeding process was nearly non-stop.

A few days later, they noticed the male hawk hadn't been around, although the female was busy tending to the two, three-week-old chicks. Then tragedy struck again when the mother did not return. Denis and Gerry learned that the female hawk was hit and killed by a passing truck when she was diving for prey. That night the orphaned baby chicks wailed and wailed.

The next morning, Denis called the local conservation officer, who immediately contacted the South Okanagan Rehabilitation Center for Owls (SORCO). Soon after, volunteers from SORCO arrived to assess the situation. The nest was fifteen meters above the ground, with no protection from the cold and blowing rain. With the chicks starving for nourishment, they knew time was running out. SORCO contacted the local municipality for assistance, but they didn't have a large bucket truck available. They called a local tree service company who offered to help but could only get there in the afternoon. For four hours, all they could do was watch and wait as a hailstorm came through, beating down on the nest and the two chicks. When the service crew arrived so did the local TV station, who were always on the lookout for a local news story. As the hydraulic lift raised the SORCO volunteer within reach of the nest they discovered that one of the chicks was dead and the other was cold and weak.

They immediately wrapped the remaining chick in a blanket and transported it to the SORCO rehab facility near Oliver, BC.

The next three days were touch and go. The young orphan (named Frankie by Denis and Gerry) was hand-fed every four hours. The initial treatment was so successful Frankie doubled in size over a

Fly Like an Eagle — Real Life Stories of Hope and Inspiration

two week period and gradually learned to feed himself.

The bird's next challenge was to learn to fly without the guidance of an adult hawk. A SORCO volunteer placed Frankie in a large flight pen and within hours he began to experiment. Although comically awkward at first, Frankie was soon demonstrating some graceful flight movements. But would he know how to hunt? When a live prey was placed in his pen, Frankie followed it with his big eyes, and all of a sudden—swoosh—he had the baby rat in his needle-sharp talons.

After about six months at the SORCO facility, it was time for Frankie to be released back to the wild. SORCO volunteers, along with Denis and Gerry, gathered in a field close to where he had been found. It was an emotional moment for Denis and Gerry as they opened the carrier door. Frankie made one long, screeching cry before flying high into the heavily treed woods.

Helping to rescue an orphan hawk was an unexpected yet remarkable experience for Denis and Gerry. It is something they are often reminded about whenever they see a red-tailed hawk, soaring overhead or when they hear its familiar shrill, screeching cry.

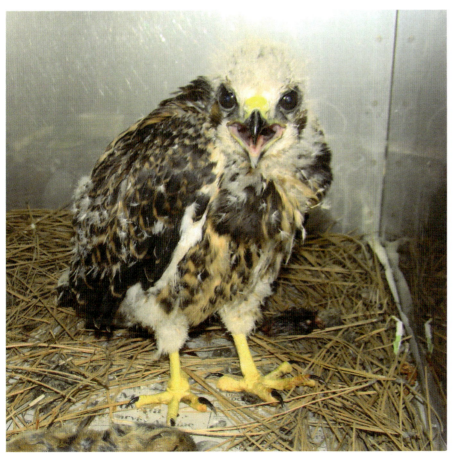

Dave Whitton *immigrated to Canada from London UK in 1968, and lived in Montreal for much of his career. For many years, Dave was a project manager for a prominent Canadian space company. He later joined an international business development team working with governments, space agencies, academia, the science community and industry from many countries. Dave retired and moved to Summerland BC in 2005. He is passionate about wildlife and volunteers a great deal of time and effort helping to develop SORCO as a world class rescue, rehab and release program for raptors.*

Compiled by Gary Doi

Teachers John Vogel and Nancy Sathre Vogel (familyonbikes.org) describe themselves as a normal, everyday, American family who happens to follow their dreams and chase rainbows. John, Nancy and their two children (Daryl and Davy) are modern-day explorers who learned early to live life to the fullest, to grab life by the horns and enjoy the ride. Together, they have pedaled bicycles 20,000 miles through fifteen countries. John and Nancy have published four books documenting their exciting adventures: Twenty Miles Per Cookie; What Were We Thinking? Bicycle Touring with Children; and Changing Gears: A Family Odyssey to the End of the World.

THE KINDNESS OF STRANGERS

By Nancy Sathre-Vogel (Between North & South Poles)

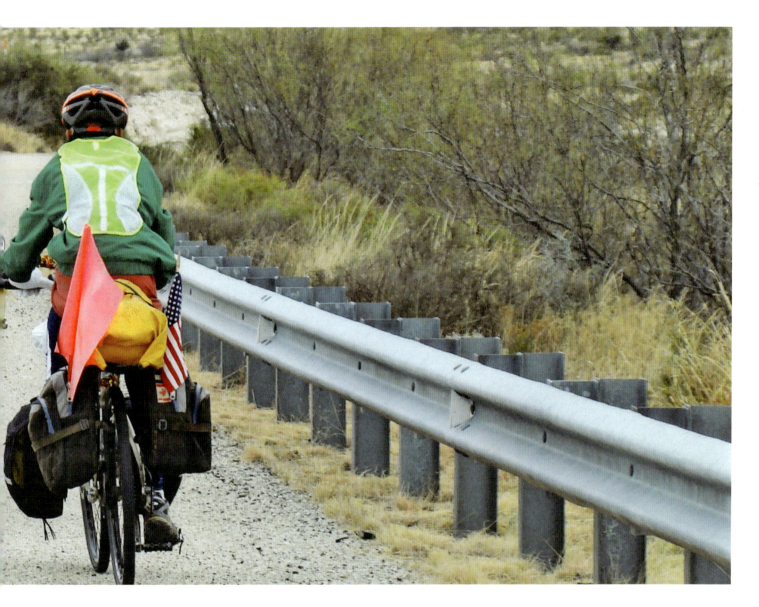

It was a long day in rural Texas. We had battled stiff headwinds for 50 miles already and were more than ready to call it a day.

For ten miles we had been searching for a spot to pitch our tent, but Texan roads are known for their vast stretches of miles and miles and more miles of nothing but empty Texan roads with fences on either side of the road.

With 5000 miles under our belts, we felt we knew the ropes. We had camped in woods or deserts off the side of the road about 150 nights already, and had never been stuck. There was always a spot for a tent hidden back there somewhere.

Until Texas.

As we wearily pedaled our heavily-laden bicycles along that long, lonely, fence-lined road, we pondered our options. Should we set up our tent in the narrow stretch of grass between the road and the fence? How dangerous would that be? Would we be able to forgive ourselves

Compiled by Gary Doi

if – God forbid – a car veered slightly and flattened our tent while our precious children were sleeping?

Mile after mile passed slowly under our wheels. The cold wind whirled around our faces, turning our noses and ears rosy red. Our fingers ached in the near-freezing temperatures.

Absolutely exhausted, we collapsed onto the side of the road as the sun made its final approach toward the horizon. "I wish a rancher would pull up and invite us to his ranch," my husband mumbled.

"That would be wonderful," the kids and I replied.

Less than a minute later, a big black SUV pulled up beside us. A window came down and a friendly face popped out.

"Where are you going to sleep tonight?" he asked.

"We have no idea," John replied. "There's just no place to set up a tent around here."

"I tell you what," the rancher replied. "Why don't you come on back to our ranch? The gate is just up here about half a mile."

Elated, all four of us piled back on our bikes and set out behind that black car. The rancher unlocked the gate, and we all bounced and jiggled down the rough rocky road back to the ranch house.

And that is how we found ourselves sitting around a table eating an enormous pot of spaghetti with Greg, Marthalynn and their four children.

As we cycled the length of the Americas, there were many times when we were invited in for a warm meal and, sometimes, a soft bed to sleep in.

In the end, we pedaled 17,285 miles through fifteen countries and we learned a thing or two through those miles. Perhaps the most important is that the universe has a way of taking care of us. Somehow – and I can't even begin to explain how this works – the universe conspires to help you.

Paulo Coelho says that, when you want something, the universe conspires to help you to achieve it. After pedaling to the ends of the world, I have to say I agree with him.

By Tara Rummell Berson (Middletown, New Jersey)

An Imperfectly Perfect Life Lesson

"Yes, Mother. I can see you are flawed. You have not hidden it. That is your greatest gift to me."

—Alice Walker (author of "The Color Purple")

Compiled by Gary Doi

During my twenties, when I'd daydream about motherhood, I remember smiling about how perfect it would be—how perfect I'd be.

We all have a sublime view of what life will look like after a big event. Some of us may be thrilled about the prospect of immediately landing our dream job after graduating, while others coo about how blissful marriage will be after their wedding day. Many of us yearn for how accomplished we'll feel after finally crossing off a bucket list item. And some of us hold the naïve view that we'll be model parents—well, at least most of time.

And then reality hits. Life gets messy. And all of those goals and moments that you thought would work out so perfectly are harder to achieve than you imagined, or aren't as amazing as you had envisioned. I've found this to be particularly true when it comes to the hard work of parenting.

I was mentally prepared—somewhat— for the transition from married life to motherhood, but what I didn't expect is how incredibly challenging daily life would be, despite that fact that everything, according to my 'life plan', seemed perfect (loving husband, two healthy kids, cuddly dog, perfect house in the 'burbs, etc.).

Since having children, there's been a lot more self-doubt...and guilt. There have been many times that I've questioned whether or not I'm a good enough person, a good enough mom, a good enough writer...or simply, good enough.

The more I've traveled this bumpy yet rewarding road of parenthood, the more I've had to let my Type A personality go; let my need for perfection go. Becoming a mother really threw me for a loop because most things have been out of my control. My life isn't just about me. My decisions and actions affect my family, and my world revolves around my kids' needs and schedules, so I've had to find a way to make it jibe—and believe me, it's not always pretty.

For example, I always thought I'd have healthy and creative meals planned for my kids, not resort to mac and cheese for dinner three times in a week because it was the easy way out. And I truly thought that I'd be able to balance being a wife, mom, daughter, sister, friend, social coordinator, homemaker, etc. along with my career without freaking out. Instead, I've ended up feeling defeated; like I'm not good at any of it—at least not at the same time.

To be honest, I've wondered whether my kids are going to end up on a couch one day discussing all the ways I screwed them up with their therapist. They've seen me sobbing in the middle of the kitchen floor or hurling a shoe at the wall over something stupid that set me off. And through my tears, I've wondered if crying in front of them or losing my cool makes me seem weak (or slightly insane). They've heard me complain incessantly about how I do everything in the house or how work is stressing me out, and in the back of my mind, I fear that I'm planting seeds that I don't appreciate their father or that I'm not grateful that I have a job.

They've seen me shovel a fistful of Doritos in my mouth and chase it with a Hershey's Kiss as a poor substitution for lunch, while I scold them for not eating their vegetables. I get angry at them for not cleaning up their rooms, but they've had to move piles of unfolded laundry just to sit on the couch. And they've heard me preach about making good choices, but have witnessed me getting pulled over by the police because it looked like I was talking on my cell phone (which thankfully I wasn't!). In essence, they've seen me during some not-so-flattering, hypocritical moments. Moments I'm not super proud of—and moments that you're probably judging me for right now!—but they're real.

While I'm busy beating myself up over stuff like this, I try to not go off the deep end by reflecting on some of my more 'shining moments'—something I highly recommend. Because despite some of the negativity and imperfections your kids will see, they'll also witness a lot of positivity.

In my case, I think about how my son has seen my face light up over an awesome hit he got during his Little League game or after he told me that he read a whole chapter of Harry Potter by himself. My daughter has seen me beam with pride during her gymnastics or dance performances (no matter how good or bad she does!), and when she proudly recites her ABCs.

My kids have seen my eyes well up whenever they turn a year older because I want to hold on to their childhood forever. They've heard me belly laugh, felt my hugs and kisses whenever they've gotten hurt, listened to my praise whenever I see them being kind and compassionate, and they've looked at each other and giggled when they've seen me kiss their dad 'just because'. And while they've also seen me get overwhelmed with work, they know that I enjoy it and that it helps pay the bills (and buys them some extra trips to the toy store!).

What I've come to realize is that for all the low points you may have as a parent, the good ones far outweigh the bad. So while I may not be a model human being or mom, all of the time, I have to remind myself that I am doing some things right. And that's a lesson you should take to heart as well.

Fly Like an Eagle — Real Life Stories of Hope and Inspiration

Something my Mom wrote to me on Mother's Day struck a chord and made me feel better. She said: "You're a wonderful mother to your children. Every day you teach them what's important in life and what's not."

Boy did that mean a lot—especially coming from my own mother who raised me well. When you boil down parenting, it's really about teaching your children about what matters most in life. It's about instilling values. And it's also about reassuring them that it's okay to not to be perfect...because life isn't perfect. So, yes, my children have seen my flaws and weaknesses, but instead of being ashamed of my imperfections, I'm showing them that you can have them and still be a good person.

You may not deal with every situation appropriately or make all the right calls. All you can do is try harder next time. Just like you learned that your life path has peaks and valleys, your kids will learn that theirs will be filled with ups and downs—and that's normal. You can aspire to have a lot more 'ups', but if you don't experience the 'downs' you won't appreciate the highs as intensely...as joyously.

By allowing your kids to see what's real, they'll learn to appreciate those fleeting, beautiful moments of perfection. They'll cherish those gifts nestled in between their less-than-stellar experiences much more because of what you weren't afraid to show them.

Photo credit: Catherine Elizabeth

Tara Rummell Berson is a writer, editor and blogger. She's been on staff at REDBOOK magazine and has contributed to numerous national media outlets. Tara also freelanced regularly for A&E Television Networks and iVillage.com and is currently a senior editor for health and wellness website KnowMore.tv. In 2011, she launched The Crankiness Crusher ™ (TCC), a WordPress blog and Facebook community. TCC is an online platform that encourages people to focus on the big and small things that bring them happiness on a daily basis and was recently featured in the book, Inspiring Hope: One Story at a Time. In addition to her editorial background, Tara has extensive PR experience and is an adjunct communications professor. She lives at the Jersey Shore with her husband, two young children and dog.

Compiled by Gary Doi

Be Great!

By Jennifer Cacaci (Kamloops, British Columbia)

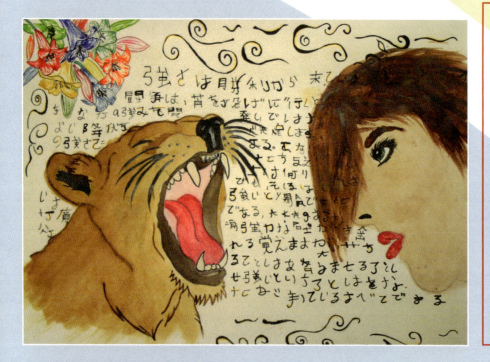

BE STRONG (Haley, Grade 9)

The lion and the lilies represent strength and that is everything my art is about. Being strong can mean physical or emotional strength. It is important to be strong physically to stay healthy and fit. It is important to be emotionally strong because when people put you down, it won't impact you as much. You will keep your head held high no matter what they say. Ever have one of those days where you just want to cry your eyes out, but you hold back you tears? When you do that it shows how strong you are. It doesn't matter what people do, say, or how they act. Don't let it get to you. We are all stronger than we think.

I stopped what I was doing and looked across my classroom, an art room crowded with teenagers. Students gathered supplies, dragged stools into place and opened books. Across the room someone knocked a bucket of markers onto the floor. There were pockets of conversation, chatter about the weekend, and laughter at some joke told just beyond my earshot. Then, almost imperceptibly, the room became calm and uncharacteristically quiet as students began to focus on the task at hand.

For the past seventeen years, I have been a high school art teacher in Kamloops, British Columbia, a job I am passionate about! My days are busy, noisy and messy. I am surrounded by teenagers and inundated with tasks, activities, and questions. While some people may find this surprising, a room full of teenagers can be quiet—if they are focused and creatively engaged.

As an Art teacher, I teach students to draw, paint and sculpt. I offer strategies for creating aesthetically pleasing

> **BE PEACEFUL (Alana, Grade 9)**
>
> My water colour painting represents my belief that it is important to be a peaceful person in our world. Being peaceful gives us the opportunity to escape from the busy world we live in and use time for ourselves. In today's society, it seems more challenging to behave as an individual. It is important to reconnect with who you really are and what you enjoy, instead of being influenced by the "cookie cutter' world around us.

artworks and encourage students to recognize the beauty in the world around them. As well, I think it is increasingly important to empower students with the knowledge that their ideas matter, that their art can communicate powerful messages.

Working closely with teens, I am acutely aware of the pressures students are under. They are navigating family problems, health issues, financial stresses, school grades— the list goes on. By the time students reach high school, experience has already taught them that life is competitive, times stressful, and circumstances not always fair. So it is understandable that teens may become frustrated and react impulsively with negative attitudes and behaviours.

I came up with the "Be Great" project to challenge students to consider "strength of character" as a theme for their artwork. I encouraged them to think about ways in which positive behaviours impact their daily interactions with people around them. In groups and as a class, we brainstormed a long list of possible ideas. Individually, students were tasked with choosing one positive characteristic to represent in a visually compelling painting. Imagery, composition, colour theory and painting techniques were all necessary considerations.

It was only a short time into this process when I discovered that "moment of silence", the moment when I knew everyone was fully engaged in the process, and creative problem solving had begun. All I had to do was wait for their visual solutions.

As this class celebrated positive human attributes, they began to see how people can choose to behave

Compiled by Gary Doi

BE COMPASSIONATE (Keri-Ann, Grade 9)

I believe that the world could greatly benefit from people practising compassion. It seems as if compassion is very scarce in our world today. It seems as though people are always too stressed in their own lives to think about other people. If we were interested in those around us, and acted with thoughtfulness and kindness, people would be happier and potentially friendlier - toward their neighbours and toward people of other nations.

differently. Rather than being competitive, frustrated, disconnected, greedy, or bitter, individuals can be generous, resilient, engaged, innovative, and thankful.

The students also recognized that by focusing on positive characteristics and behaviours, they can change not only their own experiences but enhance the experiences of others around them.

The students seemed to get it. By creating and sharing these artworks, they demonstrated that we can be optimistic about our future. Being positive and engaged in what we do is fundamental to success and happiness.

Wouldn't it be great if more and more young people (and adults) were talking about this? And then doing something about it. As if it was the most important thing in the world.

Jennifer Cacaci teaches Art at Sa-Hali Secondary in British Columbia. For more information about this art 9/10 project and others, check out (makeartforchange.blogspot.com).

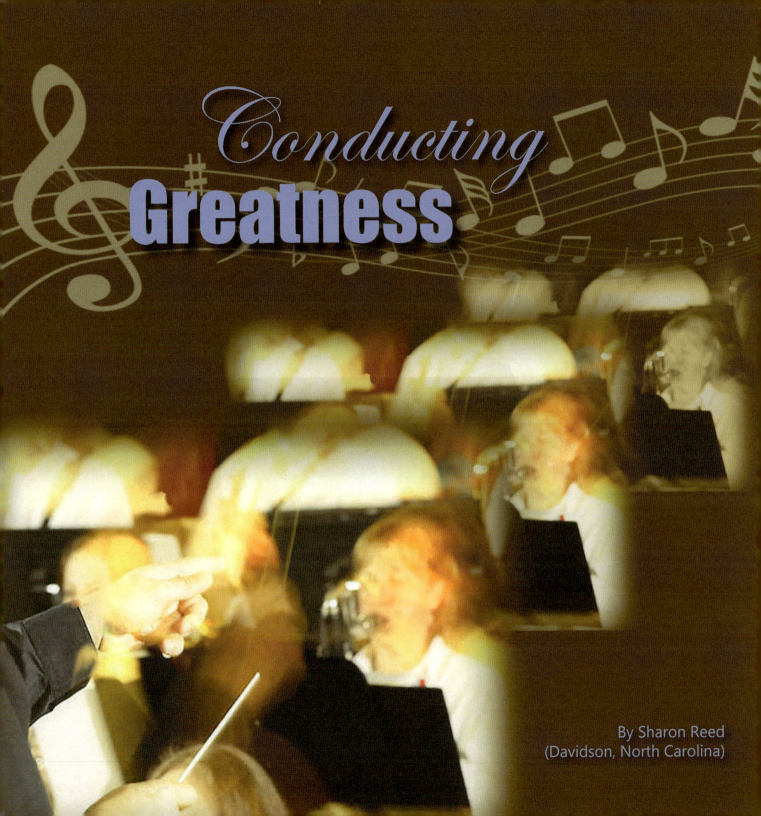

Conducting Greatness

By Sharon Reed
(Davidson, North Carolina)

This evening I attended my son's school band concert, part of a school-wide 'night of the arts'. There was a drama group, displays of visual art, a symphonic orchestra, and the beginning, intermediate and advanced concert bands. My son plays the tuba, new to the instrument after having given up the trumpet earlier in the year, in part, his dad and I secretly believe, to be closer to his friends, or perhaps even a girl he likes (though he swears it's not true).

The school itself, like many of the band's performers, is relatively new, too. Two years old, to be exact. I mention this because the school and the band are in the process of building their traditions, starting from the ground up, though with clearly defined values and a powerful vision for greatness. It is a special school on many levels, hearts and minds united in service to create a globally aware and civic-minded community of leaders and learners.

Our school's band director and her students are no exception. Tonight as I watched them perform, I couldn't help but see through a different kind of lens...not just the lens of a proud mother, but a lens which enabled me to see something more at play. Something deeper. Something richer. Something that resonated deep within.

One conductor, thirty something kids. Different instruments, different sounds, different capabilities, different tempos, different personalities. And yet despite these differences, the conductor was able to differentiate between and respond to them all. It was situational leadership 101 in action. As she prepared them to start, she knew, for example, that one was slightly out of tune, while another needed focus. She knew who needed encouragement, and who could be counted on to carry their own part. She understood that each performer had an equally important role in bringing this music to life; in creating the collective beauty of each individual note. Without them, there would be no music, simply black and white notes on a page.

A few quick adjustments made, the concert began as she smiled at her students, exuding a deep joy from within. She was, without question, leading from her heart-centered place, as I have always seen her do. With a seemingly effortless wave of her baton, she conducted these disparate parts to greatness. One crescendo here, a little more staccato there. It was all coming together beautifully. As I watched her, I could feel the momentum building. My eyes shifted away from her and to the students. Under her steady influence, they were focused, deliberate, intentional, and joyful. They knew their own part, yet had an audible vision of the whole. Practice prepared them for performance and it was clear they respected their leader. In that moment, I marveled in wonder. Not just at my son's or others' performance; not just of the melodious sounds of the band in concert, but at the poetry of leadership and teamwork in motion.

Along this journey called life, we all have an opportunity to be leaders, learners, and teammates; to work collectively together to achieve a greater good; to be a model for influencing positive change. As you reflect on this story, consider the following questions: what role(s) do you play in your own life? Are you a conductor of greatness, harnessing the collective talent of many, or do you see yourself as a performer, playing your part on the larger stage that is life? Are your choices aligned with your core strengths and values? Are they part of a larger vision? Who is the conductor in your own life?

Sharon Reed is a true third culture kid (with a grown up perspective), whose love for the world and its diversity is reflected in her work. Passionate about building bridges of understanding and empowering others to make a positive difference in the world, in 2013 she and her 10 year old daughter co-founded the Global Girls Project, a collaborative women and girls empowerment and leadership development initiative. In addition to her writing and consulting work, Sharon also serves as a UN Women Global Community Champion for women's economic empowerment.

Compiled by Gary Doi

A New Day Dawns

- Guy Tal, Photographer (Utah, USA)

Stairway to HEAVEN

By Bruce Masterman (High River, Alberta)

Ardent outdoors enthusiast **Bruce Masterman** is an award-winning Alberta writer, book author and college journalism instructor. Bruce is the author of two nonfiction books and has contributed to six others. Website: www.brucemasterman.com.

Photo credit: Bruce Masterman

The ridge has called my name for more than 30 years.

It looms high above the scenic river valley in the Rocky Mountains west of the foothills town where we live. It's a steep, west-facing slope, which means it loses snow early in the spring, and most years is carpeted by May in a soft blanket of lush green grass and wildflowers.

I've cycled the paved highway that winds its way north along the valley, and I've caught trout in the river that flows adjacent to the road. Whenever I've played at the base of the ridge I've found myself peering longingly high above me and wondered what it would be like to be way up there.

I always wondered whether I'd be able to do it, physically, or would my bum hip and knee force me to turn around partway up. Nobody likes having to turn around.

Someday, I kept thinking, I will find out. But that day never came. Year after year passed and I still hadn't climbed the ridge. Friends would regale me with tales of having done it. They'd breathlessly describe it as if it were a spiritual experience.

My response would be mixed; although happy for them, I was upset at myself for not making it happen, year after year after year. It seems I always had an excuse – too sore, too fat, too old, too busy.

On May 7th, after a winter of physical sloth and frenetic work and volunteer schedule, I was sitting in my office, watching doves and robins splash in the bird bath as I contemplated death. Not my own, but of two close friends within a week.

Both were younger than 70, and both had gone quickly. I didn't have a chance to say goodbye to one of them, and the other didn't know I was even there when I visited the afternoon before he passed.

There's nothing like death to make one aware of his own mortality. As I sat pondering this reality, inspiration struck. Today I would hike the ridge.

I quickly pack a water bottle, lunch, bear spray, binoculars and hiking poles. Less than an hour later, I stand beside the car and ponder the ridge looming high above me. I note its steepness, as if seeing for the first time how very far it is to the top. It is an ambitious first hike of the season, to be sure, but it's time. Past time.

The day is warm and sunny with a strong west wind. The first few hundred yards go well, even though I can't seem to catch my breath. I've been fighting a cold, and of course the extra pounds aren't helping. I stop often to take pictures and savour the view of snow-covered mountains and the river flowing peacefully far below. Brilliant mauve prairie crocuses punctuate the landscape.

I reach the edge of a poplar grove. A flicker of white in the trees gives away three whitetail deer, grazing peacefully just 70 yards away. I quietly sneak away to leave them in peace.

I'm serenaded by a constant chorus of Columbian ground squirrels, their voices sharp, high-pitched squeaks. Some run for cover in their dens but many do not. They watch, curious yet undisturbed, as I walk past. At the start of the hike, several golden eagles circled in the thermals above me; as I climb higher, some fly below me.

An hour later, just about two-thirds of the way to the top, I'm breathing heavily and my winter-weary muscles are complaining. I sit on a flat boulder, where I sip water and eat orange slices and barbecued elk steak left over from our supper the night before. The elk is courtesy of my friend Tom, who was pushing 80 last

57

November when he shot a fat cow near his log cabin, not 20 yards from where I tagged a whitetail buck just a few days earlier.

Evidence of elk surrounds me. The ground is indented with hoof prints and covered with droppings. I stop often to glass the openings on the ridge, hoping to see an elk. I'm also eager to see a black or grizzly bear on a distant ridge, but preferably not the one I'm on.

Continuing my slog upward, the top of the ridge is 75 yards away. But, when I get there, it proves to be a false summit, as there's yet another hill beyond it. A few minutes later, I top out. I finally made it. I can't stop smiling.

Here, the elk droppings are fresher – moist and soft when I poke them with a hiking pole. Suddenly, I smell elk. Their odour is heavy, musky, and I know they are close. I advance cautiously, using spruce and poplars for cover.

Then, there they are: four cow elk standing in a clearing a stone's throw away. Although the wind is in my favour and I'd tried to be stealthy, they've made me. Their tawny bodies are on full alert, ears upright as they peer directly at me.

On silent cue, they begin trotting, then disappear over a hill. I explore the ridge top for an hour – spying several more elk, one feeding just 50 yards away – before I find a thick fallen log to sit on. For 30 minutes, I use the binoculars to scan the surrounding mountains, ridges and clearings, and the river far below.

There are elk everywhere, small herds of feeding cows and yearlings. The bulls have lost their ivory-tipped antlers but I spy a few small bachelor herds, and one big old buckskin-coloured boy on a distant ridge. I also spot small bunches of mule deer and three more whitetails.

From my high vantage point, I inhale the clear spring air and marvel at the view. I silently give thanks for the experience, the strength to get here and for good friends and family, past and present. I have finally made it to the top of the ridge. It took me 90 minutes of actual hiking, but the journey began more than three decades ago.

And now that I'm here I don't want to leave.

Photo credit: Bruce Masterman

Trust the Process

By Francisco Little
(Johannesburg, South Africa & Beijing, China)

"Memories" - Acrylic on Canvas, by Francisco Little

The barking seemed relentless, chiseling its way into my reverie, bringing imminent surrender. Minutes stretched into what seemed an eternity. The packs of stray dogs that lived on the temple grounds were the masters of this small mountain village in the shadow of the Himalayas in northern India. Their barks made that clear.

It was a humid day and I was sitting in the temple meditation class one morning about 15 years ago, frantically swimming through the canals of my

(cotinued on page 58)

Compiled by Gary Doi

Creation

- Acrylic on Canvas, by Francisco Little

Red Dawn

- Acrylic on Canvas, by Francisco Little

(cotinued from page 55)

consciousness looking for the sign that said 'inner peace'.

The Tibetan Buddhist lama who was leading the class noticed my discomfort from his raised, yellow dias, lifted an all-knowing grey eyebrow and looked at me quizzically over the top of his steepled fingers.

"It is in the nature of a dog to bark," he said softly, without breaking the gentle rhythm of his side-to-side swaying.

As the incense smoke drifted past my vision, the ten words seemed to explode inside my head. Understanding, packaged in profound simplicity.

It wasn't a case of thinking about what the lama had said on an intellectual level, but more a case of knowing what the words meant, not only in relation to barking dogs but also to the inherent nature of life itself. People often talk about an epiphany, the golden thread that connects all things, and in that moment, in that sweaty class, I had mine.

It was for me the beginning of trusting the process, releasing the need to know and be in control of what is waiting around the corner, and being in the moment. Admittedly, 'being in the moment' has become a cliché dispensed loosely as advice by every pseudo new age 'guru' and the slogan of a thousand 'inspirational' cards. Yet it holds profound truth.

In life, one of the most daunting fears in the human experience is not being in control—the idea of surrendering for that moment to something outside of yourself. After all, how will you know this 'process' will work and why would you want to hand over control, to then be out of control? We all remember being children and playing the game with our parents where we would fall backwards knowing Mom or Dad would be there to catch us. We never doubted it—that's absolute trust. Somewhere along the way, in between the moments of love and compassion, life batters, squeezes, pushes and pulls all the childhood trust every which way. It's not surprising there are hundreds of millions of doubting Thomas's wanting to trust, but genuinely afraid to do so—whether it is in relationships, business, or any other initiative that has your name on it.

In an artistic sense I feel creativity doesn't exist within me but can be called on when needed. I think creativity in its abstract form is not about knowing what is going to happen next, it's about the opposite—trusting that the process you are busy with will lead you to its own conclusion. Show up with the right attitude, greet the white canvas respectfully (after all, it is part of the process), then be in and let go. In other words, move yourself out of the way. There is no need to know what I am going to paint—picking up the brush is the signal that taps trust on the shoulder, and says here I am, let's begin. No second guessing, no inner arguments that certain colors won't work together or designs are clashing. It's a dance—and you are not playing the music, you are listening to the music and expressing what you hear without getting in your own way. The colors already know what to do—just release them.

On my journey through life I still hear dogs barking at the most inopportune moments--but I no longer have an ideal that the world must conform to—I've learned that I'm the one who needs to flow with my surroundings. You cannot always see life close-up, sometimes you really need to take a step back, get a panoramic view, and trust the process.

Francisco Little (fjlcontemporaryart.com) is a much traveled South African born writer, photographer and artist, who grew up in Rhodesia, now Zimbabwe, where he studied Fine Art and Philosophy. He works as managing editor of an international current affairs magazine and resides between Johannesburg, South Africa and Beijing, China.

Conquering Fears Conquering Canyons

By Leigh McAdam (Calgary, Alberta)

The sudden horror of a flash flood seems very real from where I'm standing at the bottom of a slot canyon with near vertical walls on two sides of me. Escape seems unlikely. My mind's eye can picture how my death unfolds thanks to a scene in the movie 127 Hours.

Yet, I love adventure, and the adrenalin rush that goes hand in hand with it. And I especially love exploring new country—even if there's some risk involved. I am willing to backpack alone for days in bear country. Kayaking on ocean swells miles from civilization is alright too. Even public speaking to small groups is a surmountable task. But squeezing through a slot canyon narrower than my shoulders for hours on end plays havoc with my mind. Getting stuck, falling, drowning—all are deep fears though rational ones considering my circumstances.

Still I've seen the photos of Utah's slot canyons and I want to walk where few people have ever trod. I want to know what it feels like to look up at the sky when you can only see a sliver of blue. But more than anything I want that heady feeling and sense of deep satisfaction you get from confronting your fears and not only surviving but ending the adventure, with all senses engaged and the buzz of feeling so alive.

In my mind canyoneering is one big scary adventure but it's mixed with such beauty that it's a compelling combination. It is at its finest in southern Utah, particularly in the 1.7 million acres of land that make up the Grand Staircase Escalante Wilderness area. Unnamed canyons, slick rock and buttes beg to be explored. But this land doesn't suffer fools gladly. Not only is it easy to get lost in a maze of look-alike canyons, but water

Compiled by Gary Doi

is scarce and accidents can easily happen.

If you're a first-time visitor to the Escalante area, the best way to explore the canyons is with a guide. That's exactly what we did. Your guide is not only an expert in safety but has intimate knowledge of the land and the canyons you're visiting. Unfortunately no guide will be able to shut down the inner dialogue your mind is having. Ours was able to alleviate some of my worries with his quiet confidence but it was up to me to compartmentalize my fears for the day and make them manageable.

Our trailhead, like so many in the Escalante Wilderness was only accessible via a four wheel drive vehicle. On arrival at our starting point I marveled first at the beauty of the area – a burnt red mass of rock stretching for miles into the distance, but then I looked down. The dry mouth and pit of fear in my stomach morphed into a ball and started growing by the minute. I glanced at a few of my fellow adventurers and they too had *the what-in-the-world-have-we-signed-up-for* look.

The first 30 minutes turned out to be fun. It involved easy hiking down to a spot from which we could rappel 80 feet into the canyon. I knew I could handle rappelling, even if it had been over a decade since I'd last done it.

But once on the canyon floor I felt the commitment of the day. There was no way out but to go forward. Complaining would accomplish nothing either.

First I had to learn some new skills. The smear, foot-bridge, body bridge, mantle and heel plant, not only became part of my vocabulary, but they became the new found tools to get me out of this beautiful but constricted place. The heel plant ended up being particularly useful. Instead of sticking your toe into a crack you plant your heel. It doesn't get stuck

Fly Like an Eagle — Real Life Stories of Hope and Inspiration

Leigh McAdam (www.hikebiketravel.com) thrives on change and travel provides that. She has explored the world, a grand total of 53 countries. She is a photographer and travel writer in search of compelling images and stories that capture the essence of her adventures. Leigh is the author of *Discovering Canada: 100 Inspiring Outdoor Adventures* due for release in the fall of 2014.

the way your toes do. The ability to keep my feet from getting wedged between rocks helped alleviate a few of my fears.

Recent rains had left parts of the canyon very wet. A waist deep pool had to be negotiated, and there was mud so thick in places you could barely break the suction holding your foot—and all this before lunch.

My stress level markedly decreased at lunch time. A few hours of successfully negotiating slots, chocks, pools, and mud had built up my confidence. I was running on adrenaline though fear was always playing in the background. Happily the excitement of the day and the thrill of accomplishment was enough to keep most negative thoughts at bay.

Our stop at lunch time provided the only break in the entire day where the canyon opened and the angle of the rock flattened enough that it was actually possible to get out. Jim, our guide clambered up the rock to take a look at the clouds and assess the afternoon weather. He pronounced it safe to continue. I figured he didn't want to drown in a slot canyon any more than I did so let's get it done.

In hindsight it's just as well I didn't know what lay ahead. The afternoon's one mile, shoulder width slot canyon is a case in point. At times it was so narrow you had to flatten your body to get through it. I found it was better to keep moving than to think about my location; otherwise I felt the press of the walls and an overwhelming sense of being trapped.

It was a beautiful thing to come to the end of the canyon and to see a way up and out. It was more than beautiful. It was exhilarating. I felt like I'd been given another chance with life.

In the end I conquered the canyon along with a whole lot of fears. Would they still be with me if I did this journey again? Absolutely! But there's nothing like practice to increase your comfort level. I want to stay adventurous. I don't want my life to be defined by fears. Do you?

Compiled by Gary Doi

I'm a Loser & I Love It

By Arla Monteith
(Wasa, British Columbia)

It was a hot summer afternoon and there I was sitting on my patio drinking yet another pop, eating yet another chocolate bar. I had spent a long day in town and was looking to relax, to recharge my batteries so to speak. But, once again, the energy renewal wasn't happening. As I flipped through the local paper looking for something interesting to read, an ad for TOPS (Take Off Pounds Sensibly) caught my attention.

Sensibly eh? Hm? Is this what I need? My family doctor had been after me to lose weight, especially after my back surgery a couple of years earlier as even the neurosurgeon had commented about my excess weight. I was 53 years old and not getting any younger.

I started to dial the number. Nope. Can't do that. The contact person is my

neighbour. Another swig of pop and bite of chocolate bar. I was doubting myself. I felt trapped. *Yet, this could be the call that changes my life, I thought.*

I made the call. My apprehension quickly disappeared as she turned out to be *sooo* nice and friendly. She dropped by the following week and took me to my first meeting.

That first step on the scale was scary. It showed me to be two hundred pounds. *What?* I demanded a recount. Even the weight recorder was surprised. I guess my baggy clothes hid it well. She was reassuring but firm. There would be no recount. I was allowed only one visit but that was enough to convince me to sign up.

Food addiction is not something I could quit cold turkey. Yes, I could put a sign on my fridge "Visiting hours 6 am to 7 pm" or install an airbag to save me from being tempted. However, those tactics wouldn't work because I did need to be nourished. Gradually, I learned that healthy snacks—carrots, celery, nuts, fruit—could curb my cravings from the sugar-filled treats.

I loved food too much and loved too much food. Confucius had a saying about that: "Man who eat with one chopstick, never have problem with obesity." I started measuring and weighing all my food. Whether using a measuring cup or a single chopstick, I learned that portion control is the key.

I also began walking early every morning. When the pounds started dropping off, a sense of euphoria came over me. It was exercising that gave me energy, not drinking and eating copious amounts of pop and chocolate bars.

Because, input equals output, I kept a journal where I recorded everything that I put in my mouth and the amount of exercise I put out. If I lied, the scales would tell on me.

Of course, there was no magic pill. My keys to success were healthy snacks, portion control, exercise and keeping a food diary. Thanks to the encouragement and support from my TOPS chapter, I had in the past six months lost 50 pounds. For that accomplishment, I was crowned Chapter Queen and graduated to the next level, KOPS (Keep Off Pounds Sensibly). My anxieties decreased while my self-esteem increased.

The next all-important event in my life occurred when I was about to turn the BIG 6-0 and I wanted to do something special to mark this milestone. Since TOPS had helped me gain freedom from those limits imposed by my excess weight, I decided that my something special would be to participate in the Wasa Lake Triathlon. The course was a 750M swim, 20KM cycle and a 5KM run.

However, participating for the first time in a triathlon (especially at the age of 60) brought on some added challenges—for one I didn't like running. I called the organizers and was told I could crawl if I wanted. I said that I just might do that. That's when I decided to walk.

The swim was going to be my biggest challenge. I loved the water but I was not a strong swimmer and the water in Wasa Lake can be very cold in June. We were allowed to wear wetsuits so for Christmas my husband gave me a gift certificate for one. We went to the shop and after struggling to put it on, I came out of the change room.

"It doesn't seem to fit properly," I declared. The salesman and my husband looked at me and then at each other. I could tell something was wrong as they burst out laughing. I had it on backwards.

Training was important and I practiced for months—walking, cycling and

Compiled by Gary Doi

swimming laps in a pool and yes, even in the cold lake. *Brrrr!* I practiced transitioning, which is changing from swimming to cycling to walking gear, to facilitate doing it quickly.

The big day arrived. I checked in and picked up my timing chip. The body markers were put to the test making the numbers legible over and around my varicose veins. There were over 700 participants. I positioned my bike near a big sign to make it easier to find when I came out of the water.

Time for the swim. I was overwhelmed and hung back a bit as everyone dashed into the water. Up to the first buoy, I was doing okay. Around the 2nd buoy, it started feeling very lonely out there. Then someone in a boat came up to me and asked, "How're you two doing?"

"Two?" I replied. "Someone is behind me?"

I came out of the water, dashed up the beach, rinsed my feet and looked up. I didn't need to worry about my bike as there were only two left on the lot.

In the cycling rules they warned against drafting. The only draft I had to worry about was the one made by other cyclists passing me. Twenty kilometers is three times around the lake. I just finished my second round when they tried to wave me into transition.

"Sorry fellas," I shouted. "One more round to go."

I felt like a celebrity. I had the road and cheering sections all to myself.

Back to transition and I headed out walking. I'm halfway through, not crawling yet, when someone behind me yelled, "Man, you walk fast! I've been trying to catch up to you since transition!"

I saw the fellow's markings as he moved ahead of me. He was 40 years old and jogging. I was 60 and walking. I felt great and picked up my pace.

Finally, I reached the home stretch. Family, friends, volunteers, and even those runners passing me by were clapping and cheering me on. My husband dashed along ahead of me with camera in hand in order to capture the moment. ...The moment I crossed the finish line. ...The moment I had worked so hard for. ...The moment I will never forget.

Wow, I did it. I actually did it.

Arla Monteith *and her husband Rod have lived in Wasa, BC since 1971. They have two grown sons Steve (Leah) and Colin (Sarah) and one grandson, Evan. Arla enjoys walking, cycling, reading, gardening, needlework, traveling, volunteering and being a wife, mom and grandmother. She's been a Brownie and Cub leader and was a member of Toastmasters for many years. She is currently leader of her Wasa TOPS chapter and continues to challenge herself by participating in various outdoor endurance events. Arla believes that the only true wealth is one's health.*

HEAR NO EVIL

By Guy Tal (Torrey, Utah)

"But one day the 'why' arises and everything begins in that weariness tinged with amazement." – Albert Camus

I learned some time ago the benefit of accepting disagreement and not engaging in futile debates. When the dark clouds of rancor and animosity threaten on the horizon, all I need to do is to remind myself of the words of George Herbert: "Living well is the best revenge." I go outside; I go to places that inspire me and feed my soul, where I can be whole and content, independent of the mass of humanity; I engage in creative work; I gaze into the astounding depths of the universe on a dark night; I listen to coyotes and ravens and the crackling of coals; I breathe the perfume of sagebrush and pine and juniper smoke; I watch as feats of light and land transform and dazzle before my eyes. Meaningless banter on a random web site, if it even enters my thoughts, becomes insignificant and inconsequential, as do those that propagate it. But this time I'll make an exception because the topic at hand is exactly the reason I'm able to have these experiences. I do this for a living.

It is by no means a glamorous living, nor a lucrative one. At times it is a source of much anxiety and doubt. It required sacrifices and adaptation. But most importantly—it is possible. And the reason I write about it is exactly because so many pundits proclaiming (or pretending) to be "pros" are in the habit of going out of their way to dissuade others from attempting it. Whether it's outright saying you shouldn't, or the constant whining about office work and lack of time and changing business models and too much travel ... enough already.

Don't look to me for any great business insights. Success in such matters, however you define it, is as much about skill and temperament as it is about dumb luck. But, if you are willing to take the risks and acknowledge that failure is a real possibility, consider what is truly at stake: the value of a life—your life; the greatest gift you will ever be given. Are you really prepared to wake up one day, when it is too late, and admit that you gave up your dream, that you lived an unsatisfying life, that you could have been, if only … because of something you read online, written by someone you know little about?

I struggled with the decision to "go pro" for a long time. I spent years in offices and cubicles, yearning to be elsewhere. For decades I made a good living, lived a comfortable life, and patted myself on the shoulder for having accomplished the fabled American Dream. But, I was not happy. I was not fulfilled. I did not feel like I was living my life to its fullest. It made me bitter and angry. It took a toll on my health and my relationships. Like many others, I'm sure, I found myself struggling with the question of whether the celebrated career-driven urban lifestyle was really all that there was to aspire to. And, having realized the answer, I could no longer pretend to not know what it was, or that it did not matter.

There came a point when I could no longer reconcile my most fundamental notions about what makes a life worth living with the actual life I was living. I could no longer be one person in theory and another in practice. I could no longer be one person in my "off" time and another person in my professional endeavors. I could no longer be the person secretly admiring others for doing the things I wanted to do and being the things I wanted to be, rather than doing and being them myself. I had to at least try. Either that or give up hope. The scale tipped when I realized that the latter was a far more terrifying prospect than the former.

Looking back, it was one of the best decisions I ever made, though I went into it knowing it could just as easily have been the wrong one. But that's the thing about meaningful accomplishment: you roll the dice and you accept the risk and you go into it prepared to pick up the pieces and move on if you fail. It's not for everyone and it's not easy, but if you believe you have what it takes and you acknowledge the risk, and you see yourself spiraling deeper into despair at the thought of not accomplishing it, it's likely that the regret of not trying will ultimately be worse than failure.

This is not to say that photography is the one thing that can inspire such contentment, far from it. Many do find their calling in careers, in raising families, in political activism or any number of other avenues. The point is that if you want something—anything—badly enough that it hurts, and you know that accomplishing it will enrich your life beyond anything else you may do, and give your life meaning and pride and contentment, don't delegate the decision to anyone else.

Photography as a business has changed considerably in recent years. Old models may no longer be possible. If you want to make a living in it, you have to be creative not only in your photographic work but in coming up with novel ideas. I say this with the humility of someone who still wonders about the long-term prospects of being in this business, and the knowledge that I could not have done it without the unwavering support of my wonderful wife. But, even if it all ends today, it would still have been the right call and one of the most transformational experiences of my life. It has altered me in ways I could not have predicted and has made me a better person.

So, don't listen to the naysayers.

Consider your own situation, factor your own risks, prioritize what is truly valuable to you and your own aspirations, and whatever you do, be at peace with yourself and your choices.

I started with a quote from Camus, whose philosophy I admire, and I will end with another, in honor of the recent 100th anniversary of his birthday:

"But what is happiness except the simple harmony between a man and the life he leads?"

I'm the happiest person I know.

Guy Tal is a published author and photographic artist. He resides in a remote part of Utah, in a high desert region known as the Colorado Plateau – a place that inspired him deeply for much of his life and that continues to feature in his images and writing. In his photographic work, Guy seeks to articulate a reverence for the wild. He writes about, and teaches, the values of living a creative life and finding fulfillment through one's art.

Photo credit: Guy Tal

A Lifetime of Memories

By Larry Osachoff (South Surrey, British Columbia)

Photo credit: Sherril Osachoff

I'm not exactly sure how I started down this path.

It wasn't a mid-life crisis. Mid-life maybe, but certainly not a crisis. I don't recall desperate moments of hand wringing and soul searching. I didn't proclaim, "Oh woe is me. My life is almost over." If anything, I would have said, "I have a lot of good years left and a lot to live for!"

Still, I was 56 years old at the time. Five years earlier, my cardiologist had treated me for coronary heart disease by inserting a stent. He also left me with some sage advice: Don't forget to live a full life.

A full life?

I know there are times when one wonders what it's all about and whether this is all there is. I remember being inspired by my son Jason, who loved living on the edge: the adrenaline rush of skydiving, the intrigue and mystique of exploring the Great Barrier Reef and the thrill of bush camping in Queensland's spectacular Outback. Those were just some of his adventures.

What were mine?

I was happily married and had spent most of my working life developing a successful investment business. Yet, I was probably itching to do something more. Something different, fulfilling and grand.

Something like...cycling across Canada.

Biking 7,100 kilometres may seem extreme but, over two months, it was about 120 kilometres a day. That sounded doable. The more I thought about it, the more I warmed up to the idea. Yet, it wasn't the love of cycling that drew me in, it was the challenge.

Did I have some concerns about a cross-country endurance trip? Absolutely. But I planned to stay overnight and rest-up at motels, hostels and B&B homes along the way. No doubt, my body would appreciate a comfortable bed, hot shower and healthy meals. Plus, it would be a lot safer. Safety was a particular concern of my wife Sherril. I promised her we would talk each day, and she could help by providing regular updates to friends, family and business clients. I was also fully committed to maintaining service support to all of my clients while I was away. I had an exceptional assistant (with more than twenty-five years' experience) who was capable of handling all of the routine calls. She knew when to contact me for back-up on complex issues.

Still, I wasn't sure how extended periods of time in the saddle would affect me. I wasn't a competitive cyclist, but I was reasonably fit. I also had a "just do it" attitude, which meant I didn't prepare extensively in terms of training or planning. The big, unanswered question for me was: Would my mind and body harden to meet the rigours of a long-distance ride?

I intended to find out.

Departure day was June 27, 2002.

I began my journey at the White Rock pier with the ceremonial toe-dip into the cool blue waters of the Pacific Ocean. I was surrounded by a crowd of well-wishers, a few who, no doubt, thought I was a little (or a lot) crazy. That was not unexpected though, given what I was about to do.

At one point, a tall, athletic-looking woman—a complete stranger—approached me, took my hand and told me that my ride-across-Canada adventure touched her in a special way. She then presented me with a small bouquet of wildflowers.

Now, how sweet was that?

As it turned out, that was just the first of many selfless acts of goodness and compassion I would experience on the road. Kindness was the universal language. For example, at a rest stop, I met a friendly couple from Montreal who shared some wonderful road stories and then gave me some fudge and apples for my trip. When the owner of a small restaurant in Bouctouche, New Brunswick learned about my bike tour, she ripped up my food bill and told me lunch was on-the-house. Then there was the photographer from the town of St-Jean-Port-Jolie who snapped a photo for the Quebec Tourist Guide. She then presented me with a good luck charm called The Little Prince, a character from the famous French fairy tale, who goes on several adventures.

As I travelled from town to town, I soon realized the true gift of cycling. It gave me a rare opportunity to experience the landscape and culture of Canada—the treasures hidden along the roadside, the unique features of the terrain, the smell of flowers, the sounds and sights of wildlife, and the gentle nature of the small villages and hamlets. I met all manner of people who were friendly, interesting and curious. I exchanged photos and e-mails with many of them who wanted to know the outcome of my trip. Indeed, cycling provided me a front-row seat to see the country at a slower pace, without creating much impact on the environment. A travel writer said it best when he wrote: "Traveling by car, train or bus is like watching an amazingly beautiful movie go by. Traveling by bike is like being in the movie."

Oh, there were plenty of hard days too. I had to endure biking through torrential storms and scorching temperatures, climbing massive hills and cycling into severe headwinds. But I gradually learned there was nothing I couldn't handle. Like life itself, biking had its ups and downs. Regardless of the situation, it was my attitude that made the difference. As far as I was concerned, every day was a good day.

Still, the open road can be a lonely

Compiled by Gary Doi

place. I so looked forward to talking with my wife and sons each day to hear about news back home and to share my day's experience with them. It was a long-distance relationship which actually worked.

After sixty-nine days on the road (which included ten rest days), I finally reached my destination—St John's, Newfoundland—on September 3, 2002. It was a sparkling afternoon, with nothing but blue sky overhead. My colleagues from the St John's office organized the "official" greeting party at Signal Hill and they showed me the famous maritime spirit and hospitality. Newfoundland may be known as "the rock" for its rugged terrain, but it is probably home to Canada's friendliest people.

Sherril arrived the next day and accompanied me to Cape Spear, the easternmost point of North America, where I dipped my toes into the cold Atlantic Ocean. To celebrate the end of the journey, I triumphantly raised my trusty bike over my head. That was the image Sherril captured for the "journey-completed" postcard.

From St. John's, we mailed out over 400 cards to well-wishers across the country. On the back, I listed the total number of kilometres, average speed and days travelled. But the numbers didn't tell the real story.

The most important and enduring aspect of the trip were the people I met and the places I visited. For that, I can thank the many wonderful individuals from coast to coast who opened their hearts to me. I also want to give a big shout out to my team—my family, friends and clients—who helped and encouraged me on my cross-country adventure. Without them, my journey across Canada would have been an unfulfilled hope and dream. On my postcard, I summed it up this way:

"If you pedal into the sunrise, one day you will run out of road, but gain a lifetime of memories." - Larry O

Terry Fox monument (Thunder Bay, Ontario)

Larry Osachoff (larry.osachoff@rbc.com) is a Director, Vice President and Portfolio Manager with RBC Dominion Securities, Canada's largest wealth management firm. He is a successful Investment Advisor who has qualified for the RBC Dominion Securities elite Chairman's Council 28 times in his 35 year career. In 2003, Larry started a new chapter with the inclusion of his two sons, Steve and Dan, and together they manage investment portfolios for individuals, corporations and charities. Following his cross-Canada trip, Larry cycled across Europe, Russia and China during the summer months of 2003, 2004 & 2005. In total, his travels covered over 20,000 kilometres.

Larry & Sherril Osachoff

The Sweet Scent of Home

By Gary Doi (Penticton, British Columbia)

"What would you do," asked Stan, **"if the doctor said you only had six months?"**

I hesitated for a moment and smartly replied, "I'd get a second opinion."

He laughed.

Then I added, "Science writer Isaac Asimov said—I'd type faster."

He laughed again.

Village of Slocan

Photos by Gary Doi

Fly Like an Eagle — Real Life Stories of Hope and Inspiration

Truth be known, I wasn't sure how to answer a hypothetical life and death question, especially since it wasn't hypothetical for my brother Stan. About a year earlier, he was diagnosed with pancreatic cancer and given six months to live. Stan was only sixty-two, two years older than I.

Today was a good day for Stan. There were no distressing side effects from his chemo treatments administered the previous week at Virginia Mason Hospital in Seattle, Washington. This was our long awaited road trip home to Slocan, a quaint little village of about 300 people tucked in the beautiful West Kootenays of British Columbia. We had planned this outing months in advance as we sensed—and deep down we knew—this would be his last visit home.

Accompanying us on this journey were Stan's wife Betty, son Chad, daughter-in-law Sarah, brother George and my wife Gwen.

We were blessed with sunny skies for much of our drive until we reached the Castlegar corridor. As we headed north on Highway 3A, the sky suddenly grew dark, the clouds hung low and the winds started blowing hard. Off in the distance we could see a rainstorm approaching, creeping up on us while we made our way past the village of Thrums.

"Oh, look! I remember playing baseball there," Stan declared. "The backstop's gone. The field looks like a cow pasture!"

As we turned at the South Slocan junction, forked lightning flashed across the sky. In the far distance, thunder rumbled and soon a heavy summer rain began to fall.

"Wow, this is quite a welcome-home reception," I said.

Stan laughed, as did Betty and Gwen, who were in the back seat. Following behind us in the other vehicle were George, Chad and Sarah.

"Yeah, some fireworks," Stan said with a big grin. The wind and rain may have hampered our visibility, but it didn't dampen our spirits.

In 1966-67, the twenty-nine mile stretch of highway from South Slocan to Slocan was my daily commute as I completed my Grade 12 year at Mt. Sentinel Secondary. The little communities along the way popped up like names on street signs, except instead of being a block apart they were miles away—Crescent Valley, Slocan Park, Passmore, Vallican, Winlaw, Appledale, Perry Siding, Lemon Creek.

We stopped just outside of Slocan. George wanted to show us the site of the internment camp where several thousand Japanese Canadian citizens (including our parents and siblings) were forced to live during the war.

"We were first housed in the animal stalls at the PNE barns in Vancouver," George explained, his voice weak and muted by the rain bouncing off the umbrella. "Then we were loaded onto trains for the BC interior."

"That's where they built the temporary settlement in the winter of '42," said George, pointing to the expansive green hayfields bordering the highway. "We lived in tents for a few months. It was freezing cold. I remember having to walk a mile through the snow each day to the Slocan skating rink to get our meals."

Indeed, it must have been a tumultuous time. Racial discrimination was a powerful weapon spreading fear and hatred as families of Japanese ancestry were uprooted from their homes on the west coast and property seized. Then after the war, thousands of Japanese Canadians released from internment camps struggled

Compiled by Gary Doi

77

to start over again and rebuild their lives. Most relocated to various parts of Canada, some left the country and others (like our family) stayed behind and moved into the local community.

It continued to pour as we drove into town, forcing the windshield wipers to work overtime. Even though I had been back home several times since our family left in 1981, it was still fascinating to visit. Slocan used to be a place where everybody knew your name. Today, most of the people I knew had moved away, replaced with several generations of Slocanites who either had grown up in the area or been drawn there for some other reason. The village had a general store, post office, restaurant, K-10 school and one major employer—a sawmill, which had been shut down due to poor lumber markets. Like many other struggling resource-based towns, Slocan looked tired and dormant.

We crossed the bridge, a modern, concrete and steel platform which spans the Slocan River. When we were growing up, the bridge was an old wooden structure that even back then had seen better days. The constant weight of the monster-sized trucks hauling logs to the mill stripped or cracked many of the planks. The bridge also used to be a favorite fishing spot of ours. Not for catching game fish but for snagging the menacing mudsuckers, the bottom feeders advancing up-river like an invading army.

A short distance from the bridge was our first home, a two-storey house set back from the public gravel road and the rushing waters of the Slocan River. When we lived there, the house didn't have electricity, hot running water or indoor plumbing. It was a roof-over-our-heads costing us twenty dollars a month for rent. It was all we could afford. Mother was in charge of the household and she taught us

to work hard and sacrifice for the greater good. It was about "we," not "me,"—a communal effort where everyone had to pitch in with the older ones looking after the younger ones. There was plenty to do: preparing meals, washing dishes, cleaning clothes, filling coal oil lamps, making beds, sweeping floors, mending clothes, getting groceries, fetching wood and water and tending the garden. It was a crowded childhood all right and we were poor but I never ever felt disadvantaged. We learned to be resourceful, resilient and optimistic about the future. In fact, as a child, I don't even recall my parents talking about the internment years. Perhaps, it was like a deep dark secret, a reminder of the hurt and shame they wanted to push to the back of their minds.

Over the years, the house had seen many renovations and upgrades. The current owners dramatically altered the exterior with new windows, siding, roofline, side addition, fencing and front porch making it look like a genuine Folk Victorian styled house.

We drove over to our second house located next to the high school, a place we moved to in the summer of 1959 when I was nine years old and Stan was eleven. In sad contrast, the 80 year-old ranch style house was a neglected ruin. The generous-sized yard was unkempt, with overgrown trees, garbage and junk lying about and a collapsed outbuilding. The once luscious and orderly vegetable garden— Mother's pride and joy—had long ago been abandoned. The only noticeable "improvement" was a splash of grey paint over the pink asbestos board siding.

Our last stop was the beach, a place where Stan and I used to hang out as kids during the hot, dog-days of summer. As we parked the vehicles, the rain subsided and a few rays of sunlight began to peek

through the clouds as if to give new hope. Other than our group, there was not a single soul in sight. It felt so remote and tranquil. We walked along the fine sandy beach for a short while and then headed to the wharf to look out at the calm, clear waters of Slocan Lake and the panorama of the Valhalla Mountains.

The hard rainstorm left a freshness in the air. It reminded me of the times when Mother would bring in the laundry hung on the clothesline. The smell of the freshly dried clothes was like the smell of a rainstorm passing through, the smell of the sweet scent of home.

"We had a lot of good times growing up," said Stan. "I especially remember playing baseball and hockey, riding bikes everywhere and fishing the Little Slocan. Back then, things were so simple and uncomplicated."

Then he turned to me and said, "This has been a trip down memory lane. Thanks for making this happen."

I held my breath for a moment to keep from tearing up. I managed a weak smile and said, "I'm just happy it worked out."

There was so much more to talk about but I knew Stan was getting tired. The value of the trip and what it revealed about our family, our friendship and our early beginnings would have to wait.

For the next five minutes or so, we posed for group photos, using every possible camera and camera angle. A familiar routine at Doi Family gatherings.

Stan joked about how much the Japanese obsess over photography and we laughed.

And laughed some more.

It was good fun.

Just like those lazy-hazy, carefree days of our youth.

Stan's Family (L to R: Betty, Stan, Chad & Sarah)

Gary Doi served as Superintendent of Schools for eighteen years in three school districts in British Columbia. Previous to that, he was a teacher, consultant, school administrator and university lecturer. He created the magazine blog, "A Hopeful Sign" as he believes there is no greater force for creating change than hope. In 2013, he published the anthology "Inspiring Hope: One Story at a Time" to benefit a school library in Guatemala. "Fly Like an Eagle" is his second book dedicated to inspiring hope. Since retiring, Gary continues to pursue his interests in writing, golf, mountain biking, photography, travel and volunteer work.

Patience

"I'm so sorry to make you wait," the clerk at the mobile phone store apologized. In my former life the twenty minutes I had spent idly waiting might have annoyed me, but one unexpected gift I received from having cancer is an increased level of patience. It developed slowly over the course of five months of treatment where I lived with friends in Washington DC while my husband and children lived our regular life in Tokyo, Japan. I had to learn to let go of control and allow doctors and nurses to do their jobs to heal my body; I had to allow friends to help me with simple tasks of daily living, including making meals, keeping track of medications and test results, and doing all of the driving to and from appointments and treatments. Somehow the relinquishing of control manifested itself in an increased level of patience. Because my life changed so drastically, the time of treatment really became distinct from the time after treatment when I returned to live with my family. I find that my life is divided into three parts: before cancer, during treatment, and after cancer.

Before cancer, I would describe myself as having a low patience level. Running into a line to use an ATM upset me as would any person arriving to a meeting or event more than five minutes late. I often did things for my children, deeming it easier and faster to take care of it myself rather than waiting for their little hands to do things like tie their shoes or make cookies. When the kids made a mess or spilled something, I would have trouble hiding my annoyance. Even my husband, if he didn't do something precisely how I wanted it, became a target of my impatience.

During treatment I had no choices: I waited in doctors' offices; I waited for test results; I waited for people to pick me up and drive me places; I waited for dinner to be ready—I just waited. Sometimes, like with a PET scan, I had to wait while the disgusting drink settled in my system and then try to wait/relax in that ridiculous machine while avoiding thoughts about how tiny the opening really was. Interestingly, I found that when focusing my thoughts, I couldn't think about my children or imagine a post-cancer life during those times—it seemed too far away, tinged with too much "what-if?" That's where my training as a writer came in handy. I was able to work out the details of a plot I wanted to write, or ruminate on the motivation of a character. I can lose myself in fiction in a way that makes the rest of the world disappear and there's no consequence in it—no long-term significance. I could remember the ideas to write down later, or I could forget them. It didn't matter. Somehow the abdication of control, the ability to focus on the mundane and consider the inconsequential, has drastically increased my level of patience. In other words, it became an ironic circle: waiting engendered patience.

Another thing that has stayed with me since finishing treatment is an increased level of patience with people. Lousy store clerks don't annoy me, nor do slow waiters. I no longer experience road rage and wait on lines with ease. I find that I'm even more patient with my kids. I didn't see my children (ages 14 and 11) for four months over the course of my cancer treatment, and though we spoke once or twice every day on FaceTime, I missed them wildly. I have found, since being back in their midst, that I'm so grateful to be present, that often, other things that might have annoyed me in the past, take a back seat. Oh, I still get upset, but I reserve the right to do so for more important things like homework or safety rather than clean rooms or spilled food.

There are a few things, however, for which I have LESS patience. Here are a few examples: I have no patience for people who complain and have no intention of finding a solution to their problems because it's more fun to complain. I no longer have patience for people who worry about wrinkles—while everyone wants to look their best, me included, wrinkles have become a badge of honor to me—a badge of honor of a life well lived. I have lost my patience for people who drive distractedly. Just wait until you stop to text or call! If you miss a turn, don't try and cross five lanes of traffic for a correction; wait until it's safe to turn around. In the long run, what's a few extra minutes?

By Aimee Ledewitz Weinstein (Tokyo, Japan)

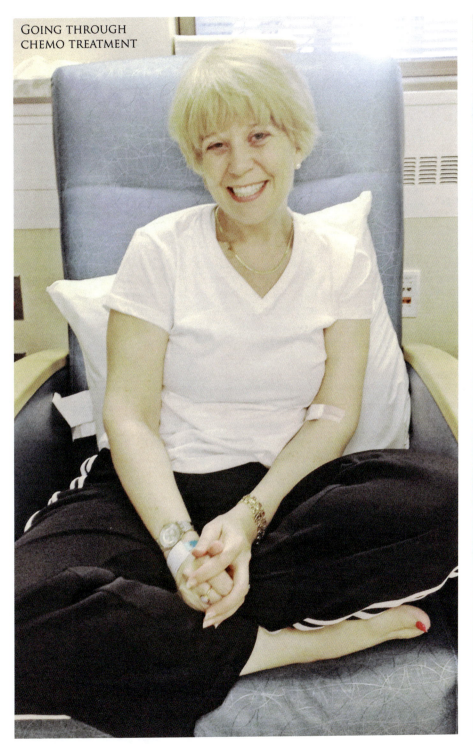

Going through chemo treatment

Before diagnosed with cancer

Compiled by Gary Doi

With Family

The thing that really gets me is people who expect other people to change their circumstances. Women who expect men to make them happy or vice versa—kids who are supposed to make their parents happy, or vice versa. Each of us is in charge of our own lives. In the best case scenario, we make ourselves happy and are then lucky enough to share our happiness with someone else—a spouse, a child, a close friend. But the happiness, really deciding to be happy, is an individual choice we each have to make every day. Some days it's easier than others, I get that. But I really have no patience for people who choose to wallow in misery or negativity. In the horrible exercise called Cancer, I had a lot of dark days, but none so dark that I couldn't get up and live my life the next day. That's my favorite mantra with my son, Bailey, age 14: the greatest part about bad days is that THEY END. Some of my friends use the mantra all the time now, too. I had endless support from wonderful friends and family, and for this I am grateful. It seems impossible to me to wallow in lousy circumstances when there are so many people who love me and wanted to help me. I have been very lucky, and lucky enough to have the ability to appreciate it.

Forgive me for sounding preachy, but I think it all comes down to gratitude really. It's okay to spend a little time mourning for the things we don't have, but the more useful exercise is being grateful for the things we do have. It has been the ultimate lesson from having cancer. We all have the power to look at our lives with gratitude and change the things that are not working for us—it might take time and effort, but change and gratitude are possible.

When I originally composed this piece, I was struggling to have patience as I waited for the results of a bone marrow biopsy. I had a clean PET scan that showed no lymphoma present, and so the biopsy, which had to be repeated for accuracy, was my last hurdle. It was one of the hardest times of all. I tried my best to fill my time with fun activities with friends and things that I love to do, including eating really good food. I agonized inwardly for five days, lived my life as normally as I possibly could, and when the results came back clean from the biopsy, the relief was so complete that I couldn't even cry. I just wanted to hug the people who shared my journey. The people to whom I looked for guidance and strength are those who helped me to understand that though bad things happen, and we might not have control over every little detail of our lives, we do have choices. Sometimes, I learned, waiting can be a wonderful thing, for in waiting and having patience, the good things can arrive in all of their faithful positivity.

I choose life. I choose to be positive. I choose patience.

Dr. Aimee Weinstein (TokyoWriter.com) *is a writer and writing professor who has lived six out of the last eight years in Tokyo, Japan. She received her doctorate from the Department of Higher Education at George Mason University and has held positions at Temple University Japan, The George Washington University, and George Mason University. She has taught a variety of writing courses, from freshman composition to advanced expository writing. Her work has been published in Kaleidescope, Tokyo Weekender, in-Touch, and Asian Jewish Life. She also maintains a regular blog where she fondly observes Tokyo life through the eyes of an American expat and writes about writing. Aimee currently resides in Tokyo with her supportive husband and two beautiful children, where she continues to write and help others in their writing.*

Frozen Fall Leaves

- Guy Tal, Photographer (Utah, USA)

Photo credit: Gary Doi

When Tragedy Strikes

By Laura Best (East Dalhousie, Nova Scotia)

It's been an emotional week in these parts. Life seems unfair when someone is taken before their time, and we can't help but feel sadness over their passing. When tragedy strikes in a small community we all share that loss. We grieve for what we're forced to accept—that someone we knew is no longer with us, taken away when they should have had many more years to live. There are two losses we're left to deal with. First, for the person who has passed, but we're also left with the feelings of how that loss affects us personally.

If you live in a small community, you can bet this person was someone you knew. Someone you shared a laugh with. Someone you came to for help. Someone you offered help to. Someone you worked with. Someone you waved to when you met them on the road. Someone whose children you grew up with. Someone who dipped you up an ice cream at the fair when you were just a kid. Someone who was a member of your family. Someone who did what was needed in the community without being asked. Someone who understood the grieving process a community goes through when tragedy strikes because they've done so in the past themselves.

Someone very recently made the comment that you, "Never hear about anything good happening." I know it's easy to go down that road when bad things happen. It reminds us then of all the recent tragedies we've heard. We don't have to go in search of proof that bad things are all around. They will find us…. if we let them. And as many times as we go searching we'll surely find those bad things….

Every day if we go looking…..
If we look for it, it's there.
But the secret is to look for good things instead. Accept the bad as a way of life, because it surely is, but seek out as much good as is possible… And it is possible… Maybe not on a particular day, but some other day it will be made possible. I understand why the comment was made. We listen to the news and are bombarded with stories that echo what this person had to say. But life is a balance. Good is all around us. So much good that it gets overlooked, overshadowed by the misfortunes that comes along.

Death comes to all of us. If we're born, we will die. There's no getting out of it. Our death will affect those around us—our family and friends, our community, people whose lives we've touched and were not even aware of. We don't get to choose the time or place or circumstances of our passing or someone else's. If this was so we'd all live forever because there'd never be a right time to say goodbye, and we'd never be ready to let go. Quite honestly, the circumstances of someone's death can sometimes be the hardest to deal with. We all understand that life is fleeting, changeable at a moment's notice, but somewhere along the way we forget that death does not only come to the old and the sick. It comes also to the young, and the healthy, and to someone who had plans for another day. In this small community we've shouldered our share of tragedies. But we face it together, feel it together, mourn together, begin the healing process together.

The sadness will lift. The memories we're left with will warm us and make us smile as we remember, a father, or a mother, or a sister, or a brother, or a son, or a daughter, or a grandchild or a neighbour.

Laura Best (laurabest.wordpress.com) has had over forty short stories published in literary magazines and anthologies. Her first young adult novel, "Bitter, Sweet," was short listed for the Geoffrey Bilson Award for Historical Fiction for Young People and made the Best Books for Kids and Teens 2011 list. Her second novel is "Flying With A Broken Wing".

Compiled by Gary Doi

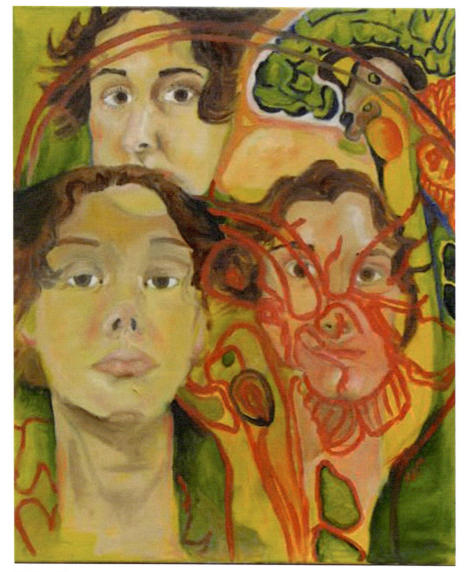

SEEING EYE-TO-EYE

Self Portrait

By Carrie Ellen Brummer
(Muscat, Oman)

Dr. S was one of them. He saw specialized conditions all over the world. "Considering, this isn't that bad," said Dr. S. He looked at me covered in blankets, trying to stay warm in my breezy hospital outfit. "Are you ready?"

I shrugged my shoulders, looked him in the eye and said, "Yes, let's do it." He blinked in surprise. Apparently, he was not accustomed to that response.

For months I complained of headaches. I kept going to a local doctor but was also trying to play doctor myself. I told her, "I'm sure it is stress related." I'm one of those night-clenchers and I just assumed the headaches were caused by biting while sleeping. I didn't think that questioning my doctor was necessary; what did a twenty-four year old know anyway? I had a strict upbringing, which included the message: "respect your elders." So, if she didn't think a CT scan was needed then neither did I. That was how it would go; me visiting my doctor every few months complaining of these headaches and being sent home again. That was how it went until the vomiting started.

Vomit. Not something anyone really likes to talk about. Well, imagine waking up every morning to vomit. Uncontrollable vomit. I would get up from bed to run to my bathroom. But when I turned

My gurney sat outside of a surgery suite where I waited for the anesthetist. I was laying on the hospital gurney in those ever so fashionable patient shirts. I swear they are made to make you feel as vulnerable and uncomfortable as possible. I also wore extremely tight stockings; apparently they help to prevent a stroke. I hoped I would wake up after all was said and done; I tried not to think about too much of anything.

Only four neurosurgeons in the world had the experience to perform this surgery;

the lights on, it felt like a gut punch and I buckled over in pain. I had intense light sensitivity. I assumed I had a bad case of the flu, called in sick to work, and went back to bed. I began to feel a bit concerned when after three days, I wasn't feeling any better. I became a hermit laying on my couch vomiting. I felt like a vampire hiding in the dark. I wasn't eating. After a week of misery, I decided it probably was not the flu. The pain became so unbearable that I finally called a friend and asked her to drive me to the emergency room.

Memory has a funny way of working, so I'm not entirely sure of the order of events. I remember a spinal tap for meningitis, intense pain killers, barf bags, and at some point a CT scan. The drugs they gave me to help with the pain (they didn't help) were so intense I hallucinated. I remember the walls melting, then looking at ceiling tiles to see them shifting around, like one of those little puzzles where you try to put the image back together.

I returned a few days later to find out the results of the CT scan. It was definitely not the flu.

"...a mass in your brain..."
"...adenoma..."
"...unknown if cancerous..."
"...surgery..."
"...Mass General Hospital..."

I left the doctor's office feeling numb. My heart was racing, my whole body tense. My emotions welled up inside as I headed home. My life could be over.

When I arrived at my apartment I saw my mother waiting for me; she had just flown up from North Carolina. I remember crying in her arms and struggling to tell her that her daughter needed brain surgery.

In fact, I don't remember much else after that. I don't even remember packing or driving to my sister's house. Much of the wait for my surgery was a blur. I vaguely remember calling my friends and trying to tell them the news with love and humor. I remember hushed voices in the house because everyone knew my head hurt. I remember hiding out in my sister's basement, where I painted. I made a makeshift studio in their carpeted basement. I laid paper on the floor to protect that carpet. I remember looking at the blank canvases I bought, wondering what to do. I kept looking at the information my doctor gave me about the surgery, which was to happen within the week. Finally, I decided:

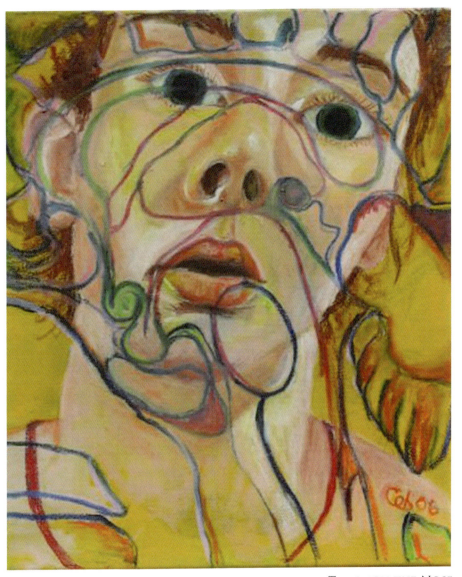

THROUGH THE NOSE

Compiled by Gary Doi

87

I had a mirror. As I painted, I noted my inner critic was quiet. In fact, silenced. And, I, Type A, was without a plan. I just made one compositional decision at a time.

In the end, I painted two self portraits during that time that helped me to digest the nature of my diagnosis. My image references? A mirror and the diagrams the doctor's secretary prepared for me to understand my surgery and the intended, and unintended, consequences. I was told I could very well lose my vision. The surgeon could accidentally nick my optic nerve and I'd never see again. I realized these paintings might be the last artworks I would ever make. There's nothing like being told you have no time left to finally lose the fear and create the way your heart has always wanted you to, open and curious.

I tried to ignore the possible consequences of my surgery running through my head... cancer, blindness, hormone therapy, death... and I painted. The arts allow you to disconnect and channel another part of yourself. Thank God for that. And it's probably for all of the above unintended consequences the doctor looked at me funny when I lay on that gurney and said, "Let's do it," like some Nike commercial. But then he nodded in this knowing way and I believe he patted me on my arm. My ego likes to remember a man impressed with his patient. I was scared as hell, but, then again, I had no choice. It left me in this strangely calm, meditative space. All I could do was accept my circumstance, and hope for the best.

When I woke up from the surgery I remember very bright lights in the surgical room and I remember feeling foggy, like something heavy was lifting up off of me. I had an insatiable urge to rub my eyes. All I wanted to do was rub my eyes. The surgical team dropped what they were doing and grabbed my arms, somewhat in a panic. I vaguely remember mumbling, "My eyes are itchy, I want to rub my eyes." Someone calmly explained that they needed to test my vision first. Perhaps that was the first moment I realized I was out of surgery and I hadn't died.

And I was SO very fortunate. My vision test came back just fine. After looking at the unknown adenoma, Dr. S discovered it wasn't even an adenoma, it was a cyst. After some time the test results also confirmed it was not cancerous. This helped to confirm my brain tumor was actually a Rathke's Cleft cyst, a cyst many people are born with but usually never grow large enough to need surgery.

My pituitary and eyes were intact. The only thing that hurt when I woke up was my stomach. They cut fat from my stomach to stuff up the incision the doctor made in my sinuses to reach the cyst. I had stitches in my head, but I didn't feel much of anything. The ones I felt were there on my belly. The nurses started teasing me, "It wouldn't hurt so much if you had a little more fat on your bones..."

Several months later, my health almost in the clear, I came across an art competition. Talk about divine timing: it was for artists facing health problems. I just barely met the age limit. And here I was, with two paintings to submit, exactly on that theme. I submitted them with a joyful, full-of-opportunity feeling. It was quite some time before I received the phone call telling me I was a finalist.

I didn't win first place. I did win a monetary prize and my work toured the United States in an exhibition that included venues like Kennedy Center for the Performing Arts and the Smithsonian. I remember flying to D.C. to be there for the grand opening and celebration, thinking I was living in a dream.

If I hadn't had that surgery, I would have never painted those paintings. I would have never experienced the freedom that comes from facing fear and accepting your circumstance. Those two paintings are my constant reminder to embrace the moment and make just one compositional decision at a time. I was empowered by the circumstance of my illness and surgery.

Prior to the surgery I had been talking with my boss about leaving the school, at which I was an art teacher. I absolutely loved my job, but many colleagues had lived and taught in countries all over the world. They kept enticing me with an "overseas" lifestyle that sounded exciting, fun and financially viable. Yet each year I was told when I needed to apply and commit to a new job and I would back out. I was scared. I could also tell my family felt mixed about it. I wondered if it was right to leave a job and place I enjoyed so much.

After my surgery my family and I would joke about challenges and say they were as "difficult as brain surgery," a sarcastic and humor-intended phrase to remind us all to have perspective. We were all a bit more grateful for life and the opportunities afforded us. It was during one of those conversations about life choices and gratitude that I finally made my decision.

After all, it doesn't take a brain surgeon to book plane tickets.

Carrie Ellen Brummer (artistthink.com) is an artist, a teacher, and a dreamer. She has been teaching Visual Arts for 8 years to students who have enriched her life! Carrie is also a practicing artist who has had art exhibits in both the United States and Dubai.

Dear Jon

By Anne Snyder (Halifax, Nova Scotia)

Looking back, you seemed to be early with most things.

It first happened when you were born. That's right. You arrived more than five weeks earlier than your due date. School had just closed for Christmas vacation. After a hectic Saturday, shopping and putting up the tree, we went to visit friends in the community of Summerland. At one point, I felt a little woozy and had to lie down for awhile as my back hurt. We were home by 9:30 that evening and I was so glad to crawl into my own bed and rest. It was around midnight when I went into heavy labour so your dad rushed me to the hospital. You couldn't even wait until morning. It was 2:00 am, December 20, 1981 when you were born. We were thrilled with our early—and best Christmas present ever.

You also skipped Kindergarten and started Grade 1 earlier than most kids, excelling in a split Grade 1/2 class. Good-humoured and helpful, you brought such joy, sometimes concern, into our lives. You spent hours out of doors, hiking with friends, building forts and even trying to 'fly' out of a tree. You delighted in your dogs and our baby chicks while growing up on Lone Hand Ranch. You enrolled in cubs, scouts, piano and singing lessons and by age 12, 'chomping at the bit' to join Army cadets. Soon, you were playing

Compiled by Gary Doi

bagpipes in the Pipe and Drum band.

In high school, you were involved early and often—keen and curious—to try your hand at many things: track and field; soccer, learning to play the alto-sax, skiing, snowboarding, rugby and community musical productions. You even made the senior basketball team—Pen Hi Lakers—owing to your tenacity and skill, certainly not your height of 5'9". Your dad and I were so proud when you graduated from Penticton Secondary School with a French Immersion diploma—one of eight boys that started in Grade 6 with 74 co-ed students.

From an early age, you devoured books on true adventure, survival, military Special Forces, and determined to become a professional soldier. You were accepted into a 4-year Royal Officer Training Program at the University of Victoria at age 17. As a result of your hard work and leadership, you became the youngest person to receive the Top Candidate award for third (and toughest) year of Basic Infantry Officer Training, graduating as 2nd Lieutenant in 2003 and stationed in the Princess Patricia's Canadian Light Infantry (PPCLI) regiment, Edmonton.

I had never seen you so happy as when you earned your airborne 'wings' (parachuting) in early 2007. Scuba diving certification followed the same year. Your career in the military took you to the Middle East, including Dubai, Abu Dhabi to train soldiers and Afghanistan on two tours of duty. Your life was full of long-distance marathons, adventure—and war.

Then, June 7th 2008 happened. A day that changed our lives forever.

I was alone at home in Halifax when I received the early evening phone call; I was delighted to see your fiancé's name (Megan Stewart) appear on call display as I answered. I was hoping she had more news about your upcoming wedding in December. But it was not her voice; it was your commanding officer. A feeling of terror welled up inside as he began to uttered those god-awful words—"Your son has died..." I remember a piercing scream issuing from deep in my throat.

To think that I had only talked with you two days earlier as you recounted a numbing event. While on a night patrol with your company of Afghan Army trainees, and four other Canadians, you were attacked on three sides by Taliban insurgents. A fierce battle of gunfire and RPGs raged for more than 90 minutes.

Jonathan's First Day of School (Grade 1)

Fly Like an Eagle — Real Life Stories of Hope and Inspiration

You were exhausted, but relieved that you and the other Canadian soldiers were able to find an escape route over broken terrain, saving many lives. A year later, you would receive the Star of Military Valour, second only to the Victoria Cross, for "courage under fire".

"How? Where?" was all I managed to say, after I caught my breath. It was then I learned you had plunged down a narrow, unmarked, 60-foot well while on a night patrol, wearing 100 pounds of gear that included a flak jacket and helmet. By the time a helicopter arrived to retrieve your lifeless body, you were pronounced dead at Kandahar Hospital having succumbed to drowning. How ironic—to drown in a desert! That night, I collapsed into my own deep 'well'. It was several years before I was able, step by step, to climb out of my shattered emotional state. In many ways, Jonathan, you were my guide.

The past six years have not been easy. Along with family and close friends, I had the support of HOPE (Helping Other Peers through Empathy), a one-on-one, confidential networking service sponsored by the Department of National Defence. After a year and a half of regular phone contact with a peer helper, I decided to join this program, undergoing a week-long training session in Ottawa.

Assisting other bereaved parents allowed me to honour your memory. In the process, I came to celebrate your life rather than become 'stuck' in your death, to follow your model: to be kind. That is what you would have wanted. You always encouraged people to lift themselves up and look outside themselves and, most importantly, to find meaning and purpose.

"He never failed to make people laugh and always enjoyed life to the fullest," your dear fiancée Megan—and girlfriend of 10 years—told me. "I know everyone will remember Jon for his military accomplishments," she said. "But mostly, I will remember the incredible person he was and how much he enriched the lives of everyone he knew."

Jon...you would be pleased to know how honoured we were when businessmen from your hometown of Penticton erected a monument and dedicated a walkway in your memory. More than twenty of your comrades attended from across Canada, including the former Governor General of Canada, Adrienne Clarkson, now Colonel-in-Chief of your regiment. She unveiled the monument, placed prominently outside the Lakeside Resort on what is now known as Jonathan Snyder Walk. I was so proud and happy—and it was a kind of epiphany—when I realized you were still so alive in the hearts and minds of your comrades, your friends and your home community. Your brother Adam, his wife Daphne, your young nephew, my grandson, Jonny, named for you, were there from Taiwan. I felt so close to you and a great burden was lifted—knowing you had lived your life just as you chose, overcoming setbacks with your calm clear logic, wisdom and determination.

In one of many phone calls from the field, you once told me: "Please do not fear for me, mum. If anything ever happens to me, I have no regrets. I am where I want to be. I am in my right place—to help train the Afghan soldiers so they will, one day, be able to defend themselves. ...The people here have so little."

You died far too early, Jon. You were only 26 years old.

But what you did and who you were in your short life was truly remarkable and inspirational.

You were early one last time, my son.

Rest in peace, dear Jon.

Love, Mum

Anne Snyder, *mother of two sons, worked as staff writer and columnist for more than a decade at the Penticton Western News. She later joined the Penticton Herald, writing two weekly columns (Art Beat and the Insnyder). She was the first to assume the position as Arts Coordinator for the Penticton & District Community Arts Council. She also served on the Penticton Leisure Service Commission, Penticton Board of Tourism and the Board of the 1995 Penticton BC Summer Games. Now retired, living on the Eastern shore of Nova Scotia, Anne volunteers with the National Hope Program providing peer support for bereaved military families. For information about this support program, contact 1-800-883-6094 or email Sophie.Richard@forces.gc.ca*

Compiled by Gary Doi

HOPE

By Sharon Reed (Davidson, North Carolina)

A warm blanket on a rainy day,
Hope cradles me in comfort
And soothes my soul,
Offering warmth and protection when life's storms blow all around.

A lighthouse amid a torrid sea,
She guides me through the dark night and the turbulent waters,
Enabling me to envision the horizon
Just beyond.

A brush on a blank canvas,
Hope paints portraits of possibility with every new stroke,
Reminding me that anything is possible, if I am willing to move forward
In faith and faithfully work toward my dream.

Heart-centered,
Purposeful and expectant,
Hope gently whispers,
"Don't give up. It will all be okay."

Empowered,
Encouraging and emboldened,
She shouts out, "You can do this!
Keep going! I'm behind you all the way!"

Our heart's hero,
Hope provides strength to endure
Or capacity to overcome,
And paves the way to purpose, possibility and the gift of our collective potential.

Sharon Reed is a true third culture kid (with a grown up perspective), whose love for the world and its diversity is reflected in her work. Passionate about building bridges of understanding and empowering others to make a positive difference in the world, in 2013 she and her 10 year old daughter co-founded the Global Girls Project, a collaborative women and girls empowerment and leadership development initiative. In addition to her writing and consulting work, Sharon also serves as a UN Women Global Community Champion for women's economic empowerment.

Laughter and Letting Go

By Carolyn Solares (Minneapolis, Minnesota)

My Grandma Flo died five years ago this spring. I've found myself thinking about her a lot lately, leading me to wonder if she's been thinking about me too. And I can't help but smile at that comforting thought.

Having been gone nearly twenty years, I returned to Fargo following a tumultuous divorce, a move marked by heartbreak and failure. Yet this detour in my life allowed me to spend more time with my grandmother in three years than I had in the previous twenty. The dynamic between us shifted. Simply put, we became friends.

I'd stay with her from time to time or drive her to appointments. Until then, I had never fully appreciated how funny she was. Yet I'm certain it was her ability to see the humor in everything that allowed her to live to ninety with myriad serious health problems. And despite her fragile health, we always found plenty of reasons to joke and laugh. When all else failed, we ate dessert. One of my sweetest memories with her is of the two of us driving around for several hours, gabbing like girlfriends while eating French pastries.

She shared many stories of her life with me, and I grew to know and appreciate her in ways I never could have as a child. When her body refused to cooperate with her mind, I'd help her into a chair or bed, and the two of us would trade a smile as she'd sigh deeply, saying "Ah, blesséd relief"—a phrase she'd adopted from her mother-in-law.

For her ninetieth birthday, a small group of us gathered at my sister's restaurant to celebrate. My grandma and I told my sister and two aunts how much we laughed whenever the two of us were together. And she lamented not being able to understand people who didn't have a sense of humor, like her own rigid mother. Then she imitated her mother's laugh: an awkward, humorless sound, one without a smile. The four of us burst out laughing at her imitation.

She further described how her mother-in-law, by contrast, never got jokes, but would laugh politely nonetheless. Making an odd sound through her nose, Grandma imitated her mother-in-law's confused laugh, causing the five of us to snort and choke on our own laughter until we were all crying.

On a lull, she seemed to switch gears, saying with a note of seriousness how grateful she was that everyone in her own family had a great sense of humor. Then, with a deadpan expression, she turned to one of my aunts and said, "Well, except maybe you."

With that, she burst out laughing again. To my aunt's credit, she handled this quip good-naturedly as the rest of us wiped tears from our eyes. My grandma was laughing so hard she had squeezed her eyes shut and crinkled her face into one of the biggest grins I have ever seen. The rest of us began another round of hysterics as she futilely tried to catch her breath while joyfully cackling with complete abandon.

Six months later, on the heels of the Fargo Flood in the spring of 2009, Grandma Flo suffered a series of strokes

that would lead to her death. "A victim of the flood," she had called herself.

During that time, I learned something precious about death and life, both punctuated by the sounds and smells of spring—and a welcome end to a very long North Dakota winter. But I'll admit the lessons felt bittersweet as my grandmother lay dying.

Throughout her life, she had always preferred to go with the flow and defer decisions. But in the days following her strokes, she was decisive and incredibly brave. With more courage than I knew she had, she declared, "I have already won the race." I remember telling her how proud I was of her for being so brave, to which she replied drolly, "It's a toss-up."

I visited her daily in those final days. As I entered her hospital room late one evening, she greeted me with a big smile as she continued to giggle with two of my aunts. For the next hour, the four of us laughed about ordinary things, which suddenly seemed ridiculous. I realized then I hadn't seen her really laugh in many months. And I began to see the energy and effort she had expended during the last year of her life, which I suspect had been more difficult for her than any of us ever knew.

But with her death imminent, she no longer had to strain and worry to make it to the next day. She could relax and simply be. And on that night, she relished every moment while laughing with her eyes squeezed tight and her face crinkled into that big familiar grin.

I can't help but wonder if I will be brave enough to laugh like that when I am dying. But I like to think that I will, because I now know what grace looks like.

In hindsight, I realize it wasn't just my grandmother's sense of humor that carried her through, but her ability to accept her situation—and everyone else too, with all of our imperfections. She appreciated, in the moment, the complexity of our family dynamics: the serious, the silly, and the sublime. When blended together with love, they made our flawed relationships somehow perfect.

Through her acceptance, I discovered the poignant freedom in letting people be who they need to be, to do what they need to do. Even if that means dying.

The morning of her death, a dozen family members spanning three generations gathered in her hospital room. We sang some of her favorite songs, and she died quietly as our impromptu family choir sang Que Sera, Sera. With the sounds of the chorus echoing in the room, "What will be, will be," my aunt looked up at us tearfully and said, "I think she's no longer with us." And I easily pictured my Grandma Flo's sweet smile and heard her sigh, "Ah, bless éd relief."

> **Carolyn Solares** is a writer, artist, business strategist – and recovering MBA. She lives in Minneapolis, where she writes about the journey of living a happy life. Visit her online at www.carolynsolares.com.

Compiled by Gary Doi

To all those who inspire hope.

Made in the USA
Charleston, SC
02 November 2014